First World War
and Army of Occupation
War Diary
France, Belgium and Germany

15 DIVISION
Divisional Troops
72 Brigade Royal Field Artillery
9 July 1915 - 31 December 1916

WO95/1924/1

The Naval & Military Press Ltd
www.nmarchive.com
Published in association with The National Archives

Published by

The Naval & Military Press Ltd

Unit 10 Ridgewood Industrial Park,
Uckfield, East Sussex,
TN22 5QE England
Tel: +44 (0) 1825 749494

www.naval-military-press.com

www.nmarchive.com

This diary has been reprinted in facsimile from the original. Any imperfections are inevitably reproduced and the quality may fall short of modern type and cartographic standards.

© Crown Copyright
Images reproduced by permission of The National Archives, London, England, 2015.

Contents

Document type	Place/Title	Date From	Date To
Heading	WO95/1924/1		
Heading	15th Division 72nd Brigade R.F.A. Jly 1915-Dec 1916 To 3rd Army Box 1924		
Heading	15th Division 72nd Brigade RFA. Vol I 9-31-7-15 Dec 16		
Heading	War Diary of 72nd Brigade R.F.A. From 9th July 1915 to 31st July 1915 Volume I.		
War Diary	Bulford	09/07/1915	10/07/1915
War Diary	Havre	11/07/1915	11/07/1915
War Diary	Ruminghem	12/07/1915	14/07/1915
War Diary	Ebblinghem	15/07/1915	16/07/1915
War Diary	Lapugnoy	17/07/1915	29/07/1915
War Diary	Mazingarbe	30/07/1915	31/07/1915
Heading	War Diary 532nd How Btty R.F.A. December		
Miscellaneous	War Diary of 532nd Howitzer Battery RFA from 1st December 1916 to 31st December, 1916 Volume		
Miscellaneous	To Headquarters 15th Dive arty.		
War Diary	Pierregot	01/12/1916	10/12/1916
War Diary	Martinpuich	11/12/1916	28/12/1916
War Diary	Pierregot	29/12/1916	31/12/1916
Heading	15th Division 72nd Brigade R.F.A. Vol II August 1 15		
War Diary	Mazingarbe	01/08/1915	02/08/1915
War Diary	Les Brebis	03/08/1915	31/08/1915
Heading	War Diary Headquarters. 72nd Brigade R.F.A. (15th Division) September 1915		
War Diary	Les Brebis	01/09/1915	04/09/1915
War Diary	Fosse 6. De Bethon	05/09/1915	30/09/1915
Heading	15th Division 72nd Bde. R.F.A. Vol 4 Oct 15		
War Diary	Fosse No. 6 De Bethome	01/10/1915	03/10/1915
War Diary	Larognoy	04/10/1915	15/10/1915
War Diary	Vermelles	16/10/1915	31/10/1915
Heading	15th Division 72nd Bde. R.F.A. Vol 5. Nov. 15		
War Diary	Vermelles	01/11/1915	30/11/1915
Heading	15th Div. 72nd Bde R.F.A. Vol. 6		
War Diary	Vermelles	01/12/1915	05/12/1915
War Diary	Vermelles (LI 3 d08 Ref. 36 c n w 1/2000)	05/12/1915	11/12/1915
War Diary	Vermelles	12/12/1915	31/12/1915
Heading	15th Div. 72nd Bde R.F.A. Vol 7. Jan 16		
War Diary	Vermelles	01/01/1916	07/01/1916
War Diary	Cauchy-a-la-Tour	08/01/1916	15/01/1916
War Diary	Vermelles	16/01/1916	31/01/1916
Heading	72nd Bde. R.F.A. Vol 8.		
War Diary	Vermelles	01/02/1916	29/02/1916
Miscellaneous	D.A.G. at de Base	02/04/1916	02/04/1916
Heading	72 RFA Vol 9		
War Diary	Vermelles	01/04/1916	16/04/1916
War Diary	Bellery	17/04/1916	19/04/1916
War Diary	Flechin	20/04/1916	23/04/1916
War Diary	Bellery	24/04/1916	28/04/1916
War Diary	Verquigneul	29/04/1916	04/06/1916

War Diary	Vermelles	05/06/1916	06/07/1916
War Diary	Bethune	07/07/1916	16/07/1916
War Diary	Verquigneul	17/07/1916	24/07/1916
War Diary	Berguineuse	25/07/1916	25/07/1916
War Diary	Fillievres	26/07/1916	26/07/1916
War Diary	Mezerolles	27/07/1916	27/07/1916
War Diary	Hem	28/07/1916	30/07/1916
War Diary	Bourdon	31/07/1916	31/07/1916
Heading	15th Divisional Artillery. 72nd Brigade Royal Field Artillery August 1916		
Heading	War Diary 72 Bde R.F.A. From 1st to 31st July, 1916. 1st August 1916. Bde Major, 15th Divnl. Arty.		
Heading	War Diary. of 72nd Brigade R.F.A. From 1st August, 1916 to 31st August 1916. Volume Number 13.		
Miscellaneous	To Headquarters 15th Dive arty.	31/07/1916	31/07/1916
Miscellaneous	To Headquarters 15th Dive Arty	01/09/1916	01/09/1916
War Diary	Bourdon	01/08/1916	01/08/1916
War Diary	Behencourt	02/08/1916	03/08/1916
War Diary	S 20 B 4.7	04/08/1916	12/08/1916
War Diary	Mametz	13/08/1916	31/08/1916
Miscellaneous	To Headquarters 15th Dive Arty Confidential	02/10/1916	02/10/1916
Heading	War Diary of 72nd Brigade Royal Field Arty From 1st September. 1916 to 30th September, 1916 Volume Number 14		
War Diary	Mametz	01/09/1916	10/09/1916
War Diary	X21c Sausage Valley	11/09/1916	11/09/1916
War Diary	Bolton Wood X 29 A 25	12/09/1916	19/09/1916
War Diary	Bottom Wood And St Gratien	20/09/1916	31/09/1916
Heading	War Diary of 76 Bde RFA. 1st October, 1916. to 31st October, 1916 Volume 16		
War Diary	St Gratien	01/10/1916	07/10/1916
War Diary	Lower Wood X18 A95	08/10/1916	14/10/1916
War Diary	IX 18 A 9.5.	15/10/1916	22/10/1916
War Diary	Lower Wood X18 A95.	23/10/1916	31/10/1916
Heading	War Diary of 72nd Bde R.F.A. From 1st November, 1916-30th November 1915 Volume 16		
Miscellaneous	To Headquarters 15th Dive arty	30/11/1916	30/11/1916
War Diary	Lower Wood X18 A95	01/11/1916	08/11/1916
War Diary	St Gratien	09/11/1916	11/11/1916
War Diary	Pierregot	12/11/1916	20/11/1916
War Diary	Contaxmaison Villa	21/11/1916	30/11/1916
Heading	War Diary of 72nd Brigade R.F.A. From 1st December, 1916 to 31st December, 1916 Volume 17		
War Diary	Contalmasison Villa	01/12/1916	08/12/1916
War Diary	Lower Wood (X18 A59)	09/12/1916	22/12/1916
War Diary	Pierregot	23/12/1916	31/12/1916

WO 95/1924 (1)

WO 96/1924 (1)

15TH DIVISION

72ND BRIGADE R.F.A.
JLY 1915 - DEC 1916

To 3rd ARMY

Box 1924

15TH DIVISION

121/6300

15th Division

42nd Brigade RFA.
Vol. I
9-31-7-15

Dec 16

Confidential

War Diary

of

42nd Brigade R.F.A.

from 9th July 1915 to 31st July 1915.

Volume 1.

Army Form C. 2118.

WAR DIARY
or
INTELLIGENCE SUMMARY.
(Erase heading not required.)

Instructions regarding War Diaries and Intelligence Summaries are contained in F.S. Regs., Part II. and the Staff Manual respectively. Title pages will be prepared in manuscript.

Place	Date	Hour	Summary of Events and Information	Remarks and references to Appendices
BULFORD	9.7.15	3am	Ammunition lot entrain for Southampton. 72nd Bde RFA	
RB	"	5.15am	B Battery entrain for Southampton	
	"	9.15am	C " 72nd Bde RFA entrain for Southampton	
	"	11.15am	D " " " " " "	
	"	1.15am	A " " " " " "	
	"		& Head Qr. Staff	
RB	10.9/15 Daytime Night	72nd Bde RFA Crossed from Southampton to HAVRE	
HAVRE RB	11.7.15		Stayed a day in rest camp No. 5. Received orders for the Brigade to move next day. 1 Battery per train	
RUMINGHEM	12.7.15	2.59am	H.Q.S. and A Battery 72nd Bde started and arrived at AUDRUICQ at 7.15 on 13.7.15	
RB	13.7/15		The other Batteries and Bde A.C. followed during the day moved to RUMINGHEM by Road. Billeting arrangements made for the Brigade by 8 p.m.	
		11am		

[Officer detailed to keep War Diary 72nd Bde RHBingham Lt.RFA]
RHBingham

1577 Wt.W10791/1773 500,000 1/15 D.D.&L. A.D.S.S./Forms/C. 2118.

WAR DIARY
INTELLIGENCE SUMMARY

Army Form C. 2118.

Place	Date	Hour	Summary of Events and Information	Remarks and references to Appendices
RUPINGHEM	12/7/16	2am	B Battery arrived from HAVRE	
RB		6am	C. " " "	
		9am	D. " " "	} Part of H.Q.
		1pm	A.C. " " "	} Par Hq A.C.
"	14/7/15	9.30pm	Received orders to move on the 14th July 1916	
			Received Operation Order No 1 G.Hq No 7 Artillery Group. Extract "72" Bde as part of Artillery Group." March under Brig General Lambart (16th Div R.A.) by following route. Rd HAZEBROUCK start 1/100,000. NORDAUSQUES - MOULLE - ST MARTIN au LAERT - Thence in a straight line to X Roads one mile SE of that place - Thence N.E. to southern edge of ST OMER - Then sharp to the Right (by the RUE du MDI) to ARQUES - Thence by Fort Rouge - South of Railway - RENESCURE - EBBLINGHEM - WALLON CAPPEL - LES CINQ RUES. Artillery to go above as far as ARQUES, then S.E. via CAMPAGNE - LYNDE.	
EBBLINGHEM	15/7/15	7pm	The 72nd Brigade RFA. completed the above March at 4:30. The weather was extremely hot. The Billeting party arrived earlier in the day and found room 3 fields for horse lines and parking guns, etc. cover for men not good, only 2 barns. Watering bad.	
RB		8pm	Received orders to continue march to following day i.e. Operation Orders No.2. Gpy No.7	

WAR DIARY or INTELLIGENCE SUMMARY

Army Form C. 2118.

Place	Date	Hour	Summary of Events and Information	Remarks and references to Appendices
EDSSINGHEM	16.7.15	12m	Reference H.A.Z.BROUCK/40.000. 72nd Bde. paraded starting from Road junction 700yds N.W. of W in WITTES and proceeded to I.JSBERGS via LYNDE - BLARINGHEM. Billeting party arrived at I.JSBERGS 12.30 and at Bre at 1.30. Billets here app'r v'y very little cover for men. Watering v. fair. Repleng from RENESCURE. 8am	
		8.30p	Receive Orders to move to position in 4th Corps Area.	
LAPUGNOY P.B.	17.7.15	12.10pm	72nd Bde. passed starting point N end of Hran. en ARTOIS and proceeded LILLERS - HAUTRIEUX - LOZINGHEM - to LAPUGNOY. Billeting party arrived 12.30. Billets w't good watering fair, Remain at LAPUGNOY	
" P.B.	18.7.15		Quiet day.	
" P.B.	19.7.15		Quiet day. 72nd Brigade w/ LAPUGNOY in reserve weekly orders to move into firing line. One Section of A Battery and one section of B Battery go up to relieve sections of 46th Battery 115th Battery rest of 1st Division	
" P.B.	20.7.15			
" P.B.	21.7.15		Quiet day. Bde all at LAPUGNOY	
" P.B.	22.7.15		Brigade still at LAPUGNOY	
" P.B.	23.7.15		Quiet Day	
" P.B.	24.7.15		Second Sections of A + B Battery go up to 1st Division to relieve first Sections. Wheel went up on 20.7.15. 1st Section of A + B Battery return to LAPUGNOY	
" P.B.	25.7.15		Offic. and Staff went up to see positions to be taken over from 47 London Division	

Army Form C. 2118.

WAR DIARY
or
INTELLIGENCE SUMMARY.
(Erase heading not required.)

Instructions regarding War Diaries and Intelligence Summaries are contained in F. S. Regs., Part II. and the Staff Manual respectively. Title pages will be prepared in manuscript.

Place	Date	Hour	Summary of Events and Information	Remarks and references to Appendices
LAPUGNOY	26.7.15		Quiet day. Received orders for 72" Bde to Relieve 7" London. Brigade (TF) RFA	
"	27.7.16		One section of A Battery 72nd Bde moved from LAPUGNOY to MAZINGARBE and came into action in relief of 18th Battery 7" London Bde RFA	
"	28.7.15		One section of C & D Batteries 72nd Bde RFA went into action with 46th Battery 115th Battery each of 1st Division. On night of 28th One section of B Battery 72nd Bde moved from LAPUGNOY - MAZINGARBE to relieve a Section of 28th Battery 7" London Bde; also second section of A Battery relieved second section of 1st Battery 7" London Bde	
"	29.7.15		A Battery 72nd Bde took over position and observing stations for 18th Battery 7" London Bde RFA On night of 29/7.15 Second section of B Battery 72nd Bde RFA moved from position with 1st Division. 115th Battery RE MAZING ARBE to relieve second section of 28th Battery 7" London Bde	
MAZINGARBE	30.7.15		72nd Bde B Battery took over positions and observation stations from 28th Battery 7" London Bde. H.Q. S. 72nd Bde moved from LAPUGNOY to MAZINGARBE and took over from 9e 7th LONDON Bde RFA. Position being prepared for C Battery 72nd Bde RFA	
"	31.7.15		Quiet day. Batteries in position against Enemy Zones	

31.7.15

J. W. Stirling
Colonel
72 B

WAR DIARY

532ᵈ How Bty
****** ~~BRIGADE~~ R. F. A.

December

1915

CONFIDENTIAL

WAR DIARY

of
532nd Howitzer Battery RFA

From 1st December, 1916 to 31st December, 1916.

VOLUME _____

[signature] Major, R.A.
Brigade Major 15th Divisional Artillery.

To Headquarters
   15th Divl Arty

Confidential

Herewith War Diary No 1 for month of December relating to 532nd Battery R.F.A

RH Bingham
Lt. Col.
fwr Colonel, R.F.A
Commanding 72nd Brigade, R.F.A

3/17

WAR DIARY or INTELLIGENCE SUMMARY

Army Form C. 2118.

Vol. 1. 532 How Battery

Place	Date	Hour	Summary of Events and Information	Remarks and references to Appendices
PIERREGOT	1.12.16		At PIERREGOT. 12 men and 2 Officers attached 370 for instruction.	6/13
"	2.12.16		1 man wounded.	6/13
"	3.12.16		Nothing to report.	6/13
"	4.12.16		"	6/13
"	5.12.16		"	6/13
"	6.12.16		Battery, men, horses and guns inspected by C.R.A. Brig Gen	6/13
"	7.12.16		Baenagham.	6/13
"	8.12.16		At PIERREGOT. Nothing to report.	6/13
"	9.12.16		1 Section went up to prelim. in MARTINPUICH to relieve 1 Section of 371. Conf. B.	6/13
"	10.12.16		remaining Section went up. Relief of 371 carried out.	6/13
MARTINPUICH	11.12.16		Quiet day.	6/13
"	12.12.16		" " Very quiet, observation impossible. Nothing to report.	6/13
"	13.12.16		" " on its whole. Lt Jewey M.C. R.A. and one signaller wounded	6/13
"	14.12.16		Very muddy, observation almost impossible. ordinary day and night.	6/13
"	15.12.16		Farrag's kept up by order of Bde HQ.	6/13
"	16. "			6/13
"	17. "			6/13
"	18. "		Shelly, quiet. 1 Signaller wounded. also 1 gun blew up now out of action.	6/13
"	19. "		Nothing to report.	6/13
"	20. "		"	6/13
"	21. "		"	6/13
"	22. "		"	6/13
"	23.		H.Q. 72 Bde relieved by H.Q. 71 Bde R.F.A.	6/13

Army Form C. 2118.

WAR DIARY
or
INTELLIGENCE SUMMARY
(Erase heading not required.)

Instructions regarding War Diaries and Intelligence Summaries are contained in F. S. Regs., Part II. and the Staff Manual respectively. Title Pages will be prepared in manuscript.

Place	Date	Hour	Summary of Events and Information	Remarks and references to Appendices
MARTINPUICH	24.12.18		Quiet day. Fired P.S. shell into ROUPART WOOD	
	25.12.18		Christmas day. Fairly clear day. Hostile artillery fairly active.	G.A.
	26.12.18		Quiet day. Nothing to report.	S.A.
	27.12.18		1st Section relieved by 1 section of 370. R.F.A.	G.A.
	28.12.18		Remaining section relieved by section Capt E. Grahame	W.A. S.A.
			Capt 632 to take command of C.70. R.F.A.	G.A.
			Capt M. MCC Williams R.F.A. takes command Battery in rest.	G.A.
WARLOY	29.12.18		In rest nothing to report.	S.A.
"	30.12.18		" " " "	S.A.
"	31.12.18		" " " "	G.A.
			Casualties. 3 O.R. wounded.	

W.N.A. Smith
Mr. Capt R.F.A.
Comg. 532. How Bty R.F.A.

2449 Wt. W14957/M90 750,000 1/16 J.B.C. & A. Forms/C.2118/12.

121/6753

15th Division

72nd Brigade R.F.A.
Vol. II

August. 15

WAR DIARY
or
INTELLIGENCE SUMMARY.

Army Form C. 2118.

Place	Date	Hour	Summary of Events and Information	Remarks and references to Appendices
MAZINGARBE	1/8/15		A/172 & B/172 continue registering. Second sections of C/172 & D/172 go up to be attached to 1st Division for 4 days. Captain EN Blood 2/2nd London Divisional Artillery was attached to B/172 and is still with Her Battery. Enemy shelled village of MAROC heavily and put a French 75mm gun our of action completely smashing it up. A.B.	
	2/8/15		Quiet day on our front. Great activities in French lines just south of our area. Capt Blood RFA (T.F.) left to be attached to 1st Divisional Arty. A.B.	
LES BREBIS	3/8/15		H.Q. 72nd Bde moved. Headquarters to Mine Officers in LES BREBIS. O.C. 72nd Bde for up command of W Artillery Group consisting of three Batteries of 72nd Bde and one Howitzer Battery B/173. The following officers were attached to 72nd Bde on this day for instruction. Lieut J. Armstrong 2/Lt Welsh Div. Artillery to A Battery 72nd Bde RFA and 2Lt F.B. Geller 2/Lt East Anglian Div Arty. to B Battery 72nd Bde RFA. A.B. A.B.	
	4.8.15		Quiet day. Nothing to report.	
	5.8.15		Early in the evening by previous arrangement all the Batteries of W Group Artillery opened fire on the same place in the Brewerie line after turning for a short time they managed to practically destroy some new work the Germans had done in their first and second line trenches. A.B.	

WAR DIARY
or
INTELLIGENCE SUMMARY.

(Erase heading not required.)

Army Form C. 2118

Place	Date	Hour	Summary of Events and Information	Remarks and references to Appendices
Les BREBIS.	6.8.15.		FOSSE No 5 in M 3 a 5.7 (Ref 1/20,000 Map 36c N.W.) was heavily shelled by enemy for some time we retaliated on their trenches and they ceased firing. C Battery 72nd Bde RFA brought their guns into action during the night. A.B. Quiet day. Nothing to report.	A.B.
	7.8.15.			
	8.8.15.			A.B.
	9.8.15.		Quiet day. Nothing to report.	A.B.
	10.8.15.		Quiet day. Nothing to report.	A.B.
	11.8.15.		Quiet day. Nothing to report.	A.B.
	12.8.15.		Enemy fired a few heavy shells into GRENAY. Pt M2 d 3.8 Ref 1/10000. Quiet see N W France. Otherwise all quiet all over.	A.B.
	13.8.15.		Enemy shelled our communication trenches intermittently during the day in retaliation on their trenches also a little during the night. Otherwise quiet day.	A.B.

Army Form C. 2118.

WAR DIARY
or
INTELLIGENCE SUMMARY.

(Erase heading not required.)

Place	Date	Hour	Summary of Events and Information	Remarks and references to Appendices
Les Brebis.	14.8.15		During the morning enemy shelled Siege 71. pr M&b 1.8₂ with H.E. put by a Battery Observation Station we retaliated on Puits 16 Mio d.5.g also every shelled our Trenches a little in the afternoon aw/l un retaliated otherwise quiet day. A/B.	
	15.8.15		Quiet day.	
	16.8.15		Quiet day. A/B	
	17.8.15		Quiet day. A/B	
	18.8.15		About mid day enemy shelled MAROC and communication Trench M10 a 3.1 Ref. 50000 Sheet 36c N.W. Hostile Observation station identified in Church ar M.11 t 6.6. Ref as above. J Battery 71st Bde Returned A/172 Bde RFA at mid night 18/19th 8/15. It exchange took place successfully A/B.	
	19.8.15		Quiet day A/B.	
	20.8.15		Enemy shelled our trenches a great deal during the day and night we retaliated each time on German trenches or Billets. A/B.	

WAR DIARY
or
INTELLIGENCE SUMMARY.

(Erase heading not required.)

Army Form C. 2118.

Place	Date	Hour	Summary of Events and Information	Remarks and references to Appendices
Les Brebis.	21.8.15		Enemy shelled our front trenches lightly all day, we retaliated every time on their trenches. AFB.	
	22.8.15		Co operation with Aeroplane attempted. Clouds too low to do anything. AFB.	
	23.8.15		Enemy shelled GRENAY with H.E. we retaliated with Howitzer on Ft M11 central Rax /50000 Shut 36cNW Ammunition all quiet. Ur about 8am the Germans put some very heavy shells w/5	
	24.8.15		GRENAY again at mid day. Enemy shelled both sides of Railway Embankment br L34 b - L35 (central Ref /20000 Sheet 36 NE) with 210cm H.E shells. 3rd Heavy Bde ordered upon to retaliate. All quiet during the evening and night. AFB	
			Quiet day. AFB.	
	25.8.15		Intermittent fire by enemy on our trenches. We retaliated also fired on houses Sur of pwits 16. Ft 10. C Ref /20000. Shut 36 c.N.W TRENCH on the renewy of the TRENCH on our right. AFB. DHqr Bty ranged successfully on Ft M11e 5.2 (w)	
	26.8.15		Some snipe on (store) by Aeroplane in the afternoon. AFB.	

P.T.O

Army Form C. 2118.

WAR DIARY
or
INTELLIGENCE SUMMARY.

(Erase heading not required.)

Instructions regarding War Diaries and Intelligence Summaries are contained in F. S. Regs., Part II. and the Staff Manual respectively. Title pages will be prepared in manuscript.

Place	Date	Hour	Summary of Events and Information	Remarks and references to Appendices
LES BREBIS.	27.8.15		Quiet day. B2/17. A/72.	
	28.8.15		A Battery 72 Bde. took over position of C/172 R.F.A. C Battery went into reserve at VAUDRICOURT. pt. N.E. 27.b. A/3.	
	29.8.15		Quiet day. A/3.	
	30.8.15		Quiet day. A/3.	
	31.8.15		Quiet day. A/3.	

5.9/15.

J.H. Stirling
Colonel, R.F.A.
Commanding 72nd Brigade, R.F.A.

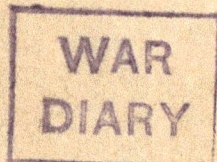

Headquarters,

72nd BRIGADE, R.F.A.

(15th Division)

S E P T E M B E R

1 9 1 5

Army Form C 2118.

WAR DIARY
or
INTELLIGENCE SUMMARY.
(Erase heading not required.)

Instructions regarding War Diaries and Intelligence Summaries are contained in F. S. Regs., Part II. and the Staff Manual respectively. Title pages will be prepared in manuscript.

Place	Date	Hour	Summary of Events and Information	Remarks and references to Appendices
LES-BREBIS.	1.9.15		Quiet day. Nothing to report. AFB.	
	2.9.15		Enemy shelled our trenches in W2 trenches very freely during the day. 1 Section G Battery R.H.A. relieved 1 section of J Battery 72 Bde. R.F.A. AFB.	
	3.9.15		All quiet during the day. G Battery R.H.A. relieved J Battery 72 Bde R.F.A. J Battery 72 Bde R.F.A. took up new positions about 40 yards in advance of their previous ones. Otherwise all quiet. AFB	
	4.9.15		Quiet day. A Battery/72 Bde. moved up W16 gun position rear. C.D Batteries 72 Bde during the night. A.F.B. W. Troop was split up and the defence of W1 section was handed over by O Commander 72 Bde RFA to C.R.A. 47th (London) Division and Artillery AFB.	
FOSSE 6. DE BETHUNE.	5.9.15		Took up H.Q. 72 Bde RFA at Fosse 6. De BETHONE. near LES BREBIS and 9 commanding 72 Bde. took up the defence of X1 Sector of the TRENCHES. Batteries started registering AFB.	
	6.9.15		Quiet day. Nothing to report AFB.	
	7.9.15		B Battery 72 Bde. took up new position during the night. AFB	

Army Form C. 2118.

WAR DIARY
or
INTELLIGENCE SUMMARY.
(Erase heading not required.)

Instructions regarding War Diaries and Intelligence Summaries are contained in F. S. Regs., Part II. and the Staff Manual respectively. Title pages will be prepared in manuscript.

Place	Date	Hour	Summary of Events and Information	Remarks and references to Appendices
Fosse No 6 de Bethune	8.9.15		We retaliated on enemy trenches for heavy trench mortar fire on our trenches in X1 otherwise all quiet. A.B.	
"	9.9.15		Enemy again fired a great many heavy trench mortars on X1 trench. A.B.	
	10.9.15		Batteries continued registering otherwise all quiet. A.B.	
	11.9.15		Quiet day. Batteries registering. A.B.	
	12.9.15		Hostile Observation Balloons prevented much forward Obsy. Retaliation was brought on enemy's trenches for Germans shelling our trenches in X1 sector. A.B.	
	13.9.15		Batteries continued Registration otherwise all quiet. A.B.	
	14.9.15		Quiet Day. Nothing to report. A.B.	
	15.9.15		Quiet Day. Nothing to report. A.B.	
	16.9.15		Quiet Day. Nothing to report. A.B.	
	17.9.15		Quiet Day. Nothing to report. A.B.	
	18.9.15		Registration was carried out over by Aeroplane for all the Batteries in the 2" Bde. Nothing further to report. A.B.	
	19.9.15		Quiet Day. Nothing to report. A.B.	
	20.9.15		Quiet Day. Nothing to report. A.B.	

Army Form C. 2118.

WAR DIARY
or
INTELLIGENCE SUMMARY.
(Erase heading not required.)

Instructions regarding War Diaries and Intelligence Summaries are contained in F. S. Regs., Part II. and the Staff Manual respectively. Title pages will be prepared in manuscript.

Place	Date	Hour	Summary of Events and Information	Remarks and references to Appendices
FOSSE N6 D- BETHUNE	21-9-15		Started wire cutting and heavy Bombardment on German front line system Ref 36000 36cNW.G34a8.7 - G28c8.2 continued all day and intermittently during the night. Progress in wire cutting very satisfactory AC3.	
	22-9-15		Bombardment and wire cutting was continued. Verma posts behind the enemy's lines were fired on. The enemy have not yet retaliated to any marked extent AC3.	
	23-9-15		Heavy Bombard was continued and by arcs to enemy's wire is severely damaged. AC3.	
	24-9-15		The Programme for Bombardment and wire cutting was carried on successfully. The Enemy have never retaliated to any extent during the Bombardment 36 par. No casualties to personal or guns have been received AC3.	
	25-9-15		*Please see covering letter. AC3.	

J. W. Stirling Lt - R.A.
Colonel 72

Army Form C. 2118.

WAR DIARY
or
INTELLIGENCE SUMMARY.
(Erase heading not required.)

Instructions regarding War Diaries and Intelligence Summaries are contained in F. S. Regs., Part II. and the Staff Manual respectively. Title pages will be prepared in manuscript.

Place	Date	Hour	Summary of Events and Information	Remarks and references to Appendices
Fosse No 6 & BETHUNE	25.9.15		The final Bombardment of the Enemy's trenches was ordered to take place early this morning. The Infantry attack took place at 6:30 am. The firing of the 72nd Bde was ordered in 4 phases, i.e. lifting at the end of each phase. The observing officers of all Batteries of the 72nd Bde RFA observed the advance of the Infantry and reports were sent on to 15" in Artillery H.Q. After a short time the smoke made observation practically impossible. At 12.30am orders were received to take 2 Batteries to the North end of LOOS. When this position had been reconnoitered it was found impossible to get guns to this position so early in the day as the German trenches had not all been bridged. One Section of B Battery 72nd Bde RFA was however brought into action just by the LENS—BETHUNE—GRENAY—BENIFONTAINE Cross Roads in direct support of 72 Infantry, this section was brought out during the night and came into action with the rest of the Battery who with C/72 had taken up a position on a reverse slope some 100 yds behind the British old front trench by the LENS-BETONE Road. A Battery and D Battery were ordered upon to move their positions on the south side of the village of MAROC. A Battery and D Battery 72nd Bde who went forward with the Brigadier General of the 46th Infantry Brigade were wounded early in the engagement and were taken to Hospital. Only 2 other ranks were wounded.	

WAR DIARY
INTELLIGENCE SUMMARY

Army Form C. 2118

Place	Date	Hour	Summary of Events and Information	Remarks and references to Appendices
FOSSE No 6 DeBETHUNE.	26.9.15		None of the Batteries of the 72 Bde RFA moved their positions from those they were in on the night of the 25th Sept. The 15th Division Infantry set having been able to hold Hill 70 the following orders were issued for the 72 Bde RFA. "2 Batteries at MAROC (That is A/72 & D/72) will bombard the Redoubt on Hill 70 with half HE + half Shrapnel from 8am to 9am. 2 Batteries in front of FOSSE 7. (B/72 & C/72) is to establish a barrage of fire along line N2 o 6.6 – N2 b 7.6. 8am to 9am Shrapnel. Ref 40000 map France Sheet 36c. Beyond this only slight intermittent firing was done. The Infantry attacked Hill 70 at 9 a.m. Barrage on the rear of Hill 70 was ordered during the night.	A3
	27.9.15		The night Barrage was stopped at 7.40 am. No Special Orders about firing were ordered. But observing Officers were ordered to shoot at any good targets.	
	27.9.15		Each day in the evening 26", 27", 26" & 9.15 went to LOOS for information of our own Infantry movements. Orders received for 72-Bde RFA to establish a Barrage from M6 d 6.7 – N2 b 27 reference 20000 map France 36c SW. in case of counter attack. An enemy gun at M10 d 5.2. observed by Capt AT. G. Gardener commanding B/72 was engaged. Ref 20000 map France 36c SW. No firing done during the night.	A3

WAR DIARY
or
INTELLIGENCE SUMMARY

Place	Date	Hour	Summary of Events and Information	Remarks and references to Appendices
Fosse No 6 de Bethune	28.9.15		Very little firing done by any of the Batteries of the 72 Bde. No change in positions have taken place. AB.	
	29.9.15		No firing done during the day. B/172 & C/172 were prepared to establish a Barrage N2 & continue to H22 d 6.5. Ref 1/20000 France 36c SW. Ref AB.	
	30.9.15		B/172 & C/172 came under command of 3rd Heavy Brigade to counter Batteries no firing done by A/172 & D/172 pending further instructions to report. AB.	

J. W. Stirling
Colonel 72' B.-le R.F.A.

10/15
2

D/7517

15th Division

72nd I.Bde: R.7.a.
Vol 4

Oct 15

Army Form C. 2118.

WAR DIARY
or
INTELLIGENCE SUMMARY.
(Erase heading not required.)

Place	Date	Hour	Summary of Events and Information	Remarks and references to Appendices
Fosse No 6 je Bette	1/10/15		No firing done by A & J Battery. B & C Battery still doing counter Battery work under orders from 3rd Heavy Brigade. AAB.	
	2/10/15		No firing done by A & J Batterys. B & C RFA. B & C Battery still on same work. Several heavy Shells fell all round C Battery 7=78de apparently aimed for the Battery. No casualties occurred. Its gun were badly damaged. AAB	
	3/10/15		All the Batteries were withdrawn to Behind Fosse 6. on the evening of the 3rd at about 6 pm ready to move in reserve. AAB	
LAPOGNY	4/10/15		The 72nd Brigade marched as ordered to HOUCHIN. Arrived here at 12 noon and received orders to go to LAPOGNY. Arrived LAPOGNY at about 5 30 pm and took up billets. AAB.	
LAPOGNY	5/10/15		Brigade in Reserve. (Lt. Sterling commanding D) n & 72nd Bde RFA took group. AAB	
	6/10/15		Still at Rest. Guns being repaired. AAB. Maj Saile au 14 then went on leave AAB.	
	7/10/15		Still at Rest. at LAPOGNY. 72 Bde He moved to Bellum AAB	
	8/10/15		MARLES LES MINES. from LAPOGNY. AAB. Bde at Rest. Still	

Army Form C. 2118.

WAR DIARY
or
INTELLIGENCE SUMMARY.
(Erase heading not required.)

Place	Date	Hour	Summary of Events and Information	Remarks and references to Appendices
LAPUGNOY	9/10/15		72 Bde RFA still at Rest at LAPUGNOY. All further leave stopped. AAB	
"	10/10/15		Still at Rest. ~~AAB~~ Brigade attended Church Parade. AAB.	
"	11/10/15		Still at Rest. Long Route march for the whole of 72 Bde RFA. AAB	
"	12/10/15		Quiet day. Still at Rest. AAB	
"	13/10/15		Quiet day in Rest. AAB	
"	14/10/15		Quiet day. Orders received to be prepared to move on 15 & 16/15. AAB.	
"	15/10/15		On night of 15/16" One section from each Battery 72 Bde RFA relieved one Section of 1st Division Batteries in the LORONS – DE RUTOIRE. AAB	
VERMELLES	16/10/15		On night of 16/17 remaining section of each Battery came into action and remaining Sections of 1st Division Batteries. Lieut. Col. commanding, 72 Bde RFA took over defence of the line of communicating 26" Bde. R.F.A. AAB.	
"	17/10/15		Save Registration carried out weather very misty. AAB	
"	18/10/15		Quiet day nothing to report. AAB	
"	19/10/15		Received orders to move Battery positions up to VERMELLES. All quiet nothing to report. AAB.	
"	20/10/15		One section of each Battery 72 Bde RFA moved to new positions in VERMELLES in 9.8.c. Ref. 1/20,000 Map France 36c N.W.	

WAR DIARY or INTELLIGENCE SUMMARY

Army Form C. 2118.

Place	Date	Hour	Summary of Events and Information	Remarks and references to Appendices
VERMELLES 21.10.15			Some registering done by Batteries weather very misty. 36th Infantry Bde were relieved in front of us by 46th Infantry Bde. Division Reviewing Section of each Battery was allowed to see position during the night of 21 & 22nd 10/15	A.B.
VERMELLES 22.10.15			Quiet day, nothing to report.	A.B.
VERMELLES	23/10/15		A good deal of Registration carried out by all Batteries of 72 Bde R.F.A. Otherwise all quiet.	A.B.
"	24/10/15		Quiet day returns to report	A.B.
"	25/10/15		Very quiet day. Some retaliation done otherwise all quiet	A.B.
"	26/10/15		Quiet day. Nothing to report.	A.B.
"	27/10/15		Registration carried out. Enemy shelled our trenches all day, all Batteries retaliated on German trenches and the QUARRIES Ref g.6.c. Trench Map 36c N.W.3. 110,000. Special firing orders from 15th Divisional Artillery by C/72 Bde RFA x Ref Sum Supp g.6.c.1.5. - 5.5-7.1 under 8 rounds per hour was 8 fired on front.	A.B. x Ref Sum Supp attd.
"	28.10.15		During the afternoon of this day the enemy shelled VERMELLES fairly heavily with 5.9" & 8" shells, some shells fell near D Battery 72 Bde RFA but no damage was done. A.B. Special firing instituted on 27.10.15 continued by C Battery 72 Bde RFA.	

1577 Wt.W10791/1773 500,000 1/15 D.D.&L. A.D.S.S./Forms/C.2118.

Army Form C. 2118.

WAR DIARY
or
INTELLIGENCE SUMMARY.
(Erase heading not required.)

Instructions regarding War Diaries and Intelligence Summaries are contained in F. S. Regs., Part II. and the Staff Manual respectively. Title pages will be prepared in manuscript.

Place	Date	Hour	Summary of Events and Information	Remarks and references to Appendices
VERMELLES	29/10/15	—	The Enemy's Artillery was very active on our support and front line trenches. All Batteries of 72 Bde RFA did considerable retaliation all through the day. VERMELLES was also shelled from about 2pm 4pm with 6.9" shells. Special Enemy ammunition on 27th carried on by B Battery 72 Bde RFA. A.B. Quiet during the day. Fire on Hostile work at 95d 8.6 – 95d 7.1 & 95d 8.7 95d 6.8	Reference Map 36c NW 3 1/10,000
"	30/10/15		at 10am, 10.30am, 11.30am & 1pm by C Battery & D Battery 72 Bde RFA at Request of Infantry. Special Bombardment of (1pm – 1.3am) & (1.8am – 1.11am) on points 96B2 – 95d 9.9 A 2 9127-8 – 96 t.52 B. in accordance with Special Bombardment Orders. 19am of D Battery 72 Bde taken forward into action at 917a 0.7 6 Fires on trench 95d 8.5 – 95 t.7.3. in accordance with Special instruction from 15th Divisional Artillery. A.B.	
"	31/10/15		Quiet day. Nothing to report. A.B.	

J.W.Stirling Colonel
of 72" Bde R.F.A.

5 11/15

72 ul Bde: R. F. a.
Vol: 5

121/7693

15th Bavarian

Nov. 15

WAR DIARY
or
INTELLIGENCE SUMMARY

(Erase heading not required.)

Army Form C. 2118

Place	Date	Hour	Summary of Events and Information	Remarks and references to Appendices
VERMELLES.	1/11/15		All Batteries retaliated for light shelling of our trenches. The one gun of D/172 sent forward on 30/10/15, known for future reference as "Lone Gun", fired on special trench. g5d.6.5 – g5b.7.3 Ref. Trench Map. 36c NW. 1/10,000, FRANCE. AB.	
	2/11/15 3/11/15		Quiet day. AB. Enemy shelled our trenches in J. Sector and VERMELLES continuously during the day. All Batteries of 72 Bde RFA retaliated on German front line and support trenches.	
			During shelling a Naval 4" gun was active against VERMELLES, shells coming from the direction of WINGLES, point H5c ref. Map 36c N.W. 1/20,000 FRANCE. During the evening considerable enemy activity having been reported by the Suffolk Regt on our B/K A/172 B/172 & C/172 fired as enemy's trenches repeatedly in 2 bursts. Lt. C. C. Russell RFA leaving joined the 72 Bde took over command of C/172 vice Major. H.W.T. ELAM. having gone home, being ill. Lieut. R. B/R	
	4/11/15		Quiet day. All Batteries fired as ordered in "FRIGHTFULNESS No. 3". ("Frightfulness" being the term given to an organised bombardment or concentration of fire on any trench, Redoubt, strong point, or area in the enemy's lines.) AB	
	5/11/15		Mr. Batteries took part in FRIGHTFULNESS No 4, otherwise all quiet. AB	
	6/11/15		Lt. J. W. Stirling, Commanding went on Gun Stay. Maj. L. Wrey Saville takes command of the Brigade. FRIGHTFULNESS Nos 5 at 6.5pm. 5.25pm. 5.50 pm. all	

WAR DIARY
or
INTELLIGENCE SUMMARY
(Erase heading not required.)

Army Form C. 2118

Place	Date	Hour	Summary of Events and Information	Remarks and references to Appendices
VERMELLES	6.11.15	all	PPA. Batteries Bde A and Lone Gun fire on Special French Mentories before Boiton 1 Lone Gun GN0.17 Ref. TRENCH MAP. Sheet No 36c NW3. PPB.	
"	7.11.15		Frightfulness No 6. at 1.10 am & 1.58 am. Houses in CITE ST ELIE. The enemy shelled our trenches a little during the day. Also sent a few shells into VERMELLES after the firing at 1.10 am & 1.56 am, otherwise all quiet. PPB.	
"	8.11.15		Quiet day. A working party of the Enemy is reported to have been caught by No 6 Frightfulness. Causing many casualties. PPB. All Batteries joined in Frightfulness No 7. PPB	
"	9.11.15		The Enemy shelled our trenches fairly heavily during the afternoon we retaliated. Nothing further to report. PPB	
"	10.11.15		We retaliated for slight shelling of our trenches. All Batteries fired on the enemy's trenches in their rearward zone in Frightfulness No 3 at 11.45am. 11.20pm. Otherwise all quiet. PPB.	
"	11.11.15		Frightfulness No 8 entered from 10.11.15 at 1.40 am & 6.10 am today. Lone Gun gun still etc. Quiet day. Nothing of interest to report. PPB	
"	12.11.15		All Batteries fired FRIGHTFULNESS No 9. at 12.30pm 12.15am (12.55am 5.50am 12.15) AA Batteries 72 Bde Retaliated for heavy shelling and bombings on trenches 96c 5½.0. — 96a7.9. Ref. TRENCH MAP No36c N.W.3. at request of the Infantry at 1.30pm. 4pm & 5am. PPB.	

Army Form C. 2118.

WAR DIARY
or
INTELLIGENCE SUMMARY.
(Erase heading not required.)

Place	Date	Hour	Summary of Events and Information	Remarks and references to Appendices
VERMELLES	13.11.15		Very quiet day. Nothing to report. AB.	
	14.11.15		Lt. J.W. Starling returned from Leave. All Batteries Bombarded enemy's trenches. Repetition of No 9 FRIGHTFULNESS. of No. 9. Lone Gun was withdrawn from advanced position and Group Battery to the Battery (J/172) AB.	
	15.11.15		Batteries carried out rapid Bombardment by order at 3pm 4pm. also on the enemy's trenches round the QUARRIES. Ref TRENCH MAP 36c N.W. 1. 96e. and 91a. at 4.45 B/172 and D/172 retaliated for enemy shelling our support trenches. AB.	
	16.11.15		Batteries carried out Bombardment by order at 10am 12noon 3.15pm of Front line communication and support trenches on their Normal Zones. Otherwise all quiet. AB	
	17.11.15		Repeated Bombardment as 16.11.15 at 9.30am 12 noon 3.15pm. All Batteries retaliated for enemy shelling our support and communication trenches. AB	
	18.11.15		No 10 FRIGHTFULNESS On enemy's line from H.1.d.0.5 — H.1.a central. Reference TRENCH MAP. No 36c N.W. at 7.15 pm for 4 minutes & shrapnel 5.11pm. The enemy retaliated rather vigorously for a few minutes, otherwise all quiet. AB.	
	19.11.15		Quiet day Nothing to report AB.	

Army Form C. 2118

WAR DIARY
INTELLIGENCE SUMMARY.
(Erase heading not required.)

Instructions regarding War Diaries and Intelligence Summaries are contained in F. S. Regs., Part II. and the Staff Manual respectively. Title pages will be prepared in manuscript.

Place	Date	Hour	Summary of Events and Information	Remarks and references to Appendices
VERMELLES.	20.11.15		FRIGHTFULNESS No 11 carried out by all Batteries 72 Bde. RFA. at 11.10 am. and 10.20 pm. This was repeated at 11.30 for enemy's retaliation. The Enemy shelled our lines pretty heavily from 11.55 am – 12.30 pm and again later in the afternoon we retaliated each time.	RF3.
"	21.11.15		Quiet day. Frenchmen No 1.2. at 2.40 pm Bombardment of houses G 6 c 8.4 & G 6 d 9.9. Ref TrenchMap No 36 c N.W.) carried out by all Batteries. Very Quiet day. Nothing to report.	RF3. RF3.
"	22.11.15			
"	23.11.15		The Zone for defence having been altered for the 72 Bde. all the Batteries were registering in new lines. The Brigade Zone now is from G12 c 3.4 to G5d 9.7. This is split up in the Brigade as follows. A/172. & B/172 forming Right & Brigade cover the line from G12 b 2.9. to G6 c 7.0 inclusive C/172 & D/172 forming Left½ Brigade cover the line G 6 c 7.0 to G 5 d 9.7 inclusive. None of the Batteries are Bde. H.Q. have had to change their positions.	RF3. RF3.
"	24.11.15		Quiet day. Batteries still registering new Zones. 3 Officers were attached as follows. 2/Lt 3.G.Laurie from 174 Bde 39 Div to A/172. 2/Lt F.T. Macaulay from 179 Bde 39 Div to D/172 2/Lt A.C. Doney 176 Div to C/172. The above officers were attached for 14 days course.	RF3. RF3.

1577 Wt.W10791/1773 500,000 1/15 D. D. & L. A.D.S.S./Forms/C. 2118.

WAR DIARY
or
INTELLIGENCE SUMMARY

Army Form C. 2118

Place	Date	Hour	Summary of Events and Information	Remarks and references to Appendices
VERMELLES	25.11.15		The enemy's artillery was fairly active against our support trenches during the day. All Batteries retaliated. AA3.	
	26.11.15		Quiet day. Nothing to report. AA3.	
	27.11.15		A bombardment of Hessulu from 9.6.c.3.7, 9.6.a.0.7, 9.6.c.3.3, 9.5.t.6.7 by A(3rd) Batteries respectively was carried out at 12 noon to 6.15am on 28/11/15. Reference Trench Map 36C N.W.1. Otherwise all quiet. AA3.	
	28.11.15		HAISNES CHURCH was registered by all Batteries 72 BAC by order of 15th DA also at 11.30am a "hot attack" average was sent through all Batteries fired on their quickfire line. 2 Batteries got their rounds off visitors or orunds of receipt of order. These were A & D Batteries. We retaliated during the day for slight shelling of our trenches. AA3	
	29.11.15		Quiet day. Nothing to report. AA3	
	30.11.15		Frightfulness No 10 Bombardment of town HAISNES Road from H7a central and from HKC centre all Batteries. The enemy did not retaliate for this shelling. AA3.	

J.M. Stirling Colonel
72 B.A.A.

1577 Wt. W10791/1773 500,000 1/15 D.D.&L. A.D.S.S./Forms/C. 2118.

72nd Bde, R.F.A.
fol. 6

76/1910

15th/7/10

Army Form C. 2118.

WAR DIARY
or
INTELLIGENCE SUMMARY.
(Erase heading not required.)

Instructions regarding War Diaries and Intelligence Summaries are contained in F. S. Regs., Part II. and the Staff Manual respectively. Title pages will be prepared in manuscript.

Place	Date	Hour	Summary of Events and Information	Remarks and references to Appendices
VERMELLES	1/12/15		During the morning the enemy shelled PHILOSOPHE & FOSSE No 3 slightly also the communication and support trenches in C1 & C2 Sec tor. In each of the cases all Batteries 72 Bde. retaliated on the GORRIES (96c) and CITÉ ST ELIE. No Batteries carried out FRIGHTFULNESS No 15. 12 rounds H.E. at 6.10 pm 10.20 pm and noon on 2.12.15. Searching took place from a line A29 d 0 5 0 - A29 c 6 5 3 by fifties.	Trench map 36c N.W.
	2.12.15		The enemy shelled our trenches slightly during today. During the morning A/72 & B/72 bombarded points in the enemy's lines which are suspected machine gun emplacements. at points 9.12 b 35 4 , 9.26-2.6* taken by A Battery and 9.20.5.2.6.6* taken by B Battery. Many direct hits were obtained, but no question gens front although considerable damage was done to the enemy's trenches A/72B. Quiet day. FRIGHTFULNESS No 17 carried out - A/72 Hie enfilade searching North B/72 B25a 4 0 Searchin South. C/72 9.6 1.40 Searchin South. at 9.30 pm. 20 shrapnel each B/3	Ret. Someone hurt on Army -
	3.12.15			
	4.12.15		Slight Shelling of PHILOSOPHE during the morning otherwise all quiet. B/3	
	5.12.15		Enemy shelled our trenches during the day for which we retaliated. at 1.30pm and 2.35 pm all Batteries in conjunction with the Heavies and other Brigades	

WAR DIARY
INTELLIGENCE SUMMARY.
(Erase heading not required.)

Army Form C. 2118.

Place	Date	Hour	Summary of Events and Information	Remarks and references to Appendices
VERMELLES (L13c08 Ref 36cN.W.1/20000)	5.12.15		Carried out heavy bombardment of the QUARRIES Ref 9 6cm 36cN.W.1 /10000 TRENCH MAP) A43	A43
	6.12.15		Slight shelling of our trenches by the enemy otherwise all quiet A43	
	7.12.15		During the morning A172 Bombarded the Winding Gear of Puits 13, in conjunction this Howitzer Enemy shelled our Trenches pretty briskly during the latter part of the afternoon. At 2.15pm & 2.45 all Batteries carried heavy bombardment of the enemy's trenches on their ordinary night lines. A43	
	8.12.15		B Battery 72 Bde Let one gun forward to LE ROUTOIRE. 91st. Ref Trench heap 36cN.W. in order to Bombard B19, W111E15 French Quiet Day. A43	
	9.12.15		Fairly heavy shelling of our trenches during the morning answered in retaliation Special Bombardment by all Batteries of CROSS TRENCH FRYSLIPE EYERS No. 20 at G4B2.5 – G502151 otherwise all quiet A43	
	10.12.15		Enemy shelled our trenches heavily throughout the day A43 Special Bombardment of trenches at back of Cité St ELIE at	
	11.12.15		Special Bombardment of houses at the back of CITÉ ST ELIE. at 4.40am 5.30am they 2 Batteries working a/t a time. 12 Shrapnel 12 HE each time Fryshulpen No 21 Enemy shelled VERMELLES and PHILOSOPHE slightly at 3.30 pm.	

WAR DIARY or INTELLIGENCE SUMMARY

Army Form C. 2118.

Place	Date	Hour	Summary of Events and Information	Remarks and references to Appendices
VERMELLES	12.12.15		At 12.30am this awning received S.O.S. signal from 1st Division on our left. A/172 e C/172 opened fire at once. A/172 in trench in front of Loss of 1st Division and C/172 on higher ining. All was quiet within a few minutes. At 12am day LeRutoir Gun shelled Big Willie doing considerable damage. At 9am all Batteries carried out FRIGHTFULNESS No 22 viz Bombardment of the JUMP and Fosche Avenue up to. RAB.	
	13.12.15		At 6am & 7.30. All Batteries fired in Frightfulness No 23 viz Bombardment of Enemy second line trenches just in front of CITÉ ST. ELIE and at 9.30am and 10am FRIGHTFULNESS No 16 Bombardment Nine. A30a0.1 – A30a2.1. Ref. Trench Map 36 N.W.1. At 7.0 to 8pm again Bombarded Big Willie doing damage. RAB.	
	14.12.15		Le Rutoir Gun at 3/172 again Bombarded Big Willie doing damage. RAB.	
	15.12.15		QUIET DAY. Nothing to report.	
	16.12.15		The 15th Divisional Artillery was relieved by 47th (London) Divisional Artillery. All Brigades of 15th Divisional Artillery went 5am to 2am. 72 Bde RFA remain in position and come under orders of C.R.A. 47th (London) Divisional Artillery and at 4.30pm to 8AM continue to cover our same zones as before. Slight shelling of our trenches during the evening. All Batteries retaliated &c.	

WAR DIARY
INTELLIGENCE SUMMARY

Army Form C. 2118.

Place	Date	Hour	Summary of Events and Information	Remarks and references to Appendices
VERMELLES	17.12.15		At 12.50am this enemy Batteries were called upon to fire by the Infantry. The Enemy made a fairly determined attack on the Essex Trench at 11.45pm (16.12.15) C/172 & D/172 fired on Enemy lines. The fire is reported to have stopped the enemy's attack and he returned to his own lines. A/B	
	18.12.15		The enemy's Artillery was very active on our trenches throughout the day. All Batteries 72nd Bde RFA fired a good deal in retaliation. A/B	
	19.12.15		Quiet Day. Enemy's Artillery fairly active all Batteries retaliated. During the night a "Special Bombardment" of Cite St Elie took place. A/B at 7.30	
	20.12.15		At 7.10am this morning the enemy made a small part of our of the trenches in our zone. C/172 & D/172 opened fire at once but the enemy could not be driven out again. Counter attacks were made during the night all Batteries of 72nd Bde fired heavily. Total expenditure of ammunition during the day of about 3000 rounds. A/B	
	21.12.15		The Bombardment of the German Lines was kept up all day by all Batteries. 2 Batteries of 72nd Bde firing at a time. A/B	

WAR DIARY
INTELLIGENCE SUMMARY.

Army Form C. 2118.

Place	Date	Hour	Summary of Events and Information	Remarks and references to Appendices
VERMELLES	22.12.15		News having been received that the enemy had a mine ready to explode a slow bombardment was kept up & Batteries firing at a time all Batteries being ready to retaliate to a barrage if required. RA3.	
	23.12.15		Bombardment continued RA3	
	24.12.15		At 7.20 am our own counter mine was exploded under the enemy's line all Batteries opened a rapid rate of fire on the enemy's front line and second line system. Fire was slowed down again to a slow bombardment RA3	
	25.12.15		CHRISTMAS DAY: A very slow fire was kept up on the enemy's trenches. Otherwise all quiet. RA3	
	26.12.15 27.12.15		QUIET DAY. An automatic Belt thrower was silenced by C/172 Nth QUARRIES RA3. On the night of 27/28 the section of each Battery and Bde. Am. Col. was relieved by sections of the 16th Div. Arty 2nd East Anglian Bde. RFA. T.F. Relief complete about 5pm. Thereafter all guns RA3	
	28.12.15		The enemy's Artillery was active against our trenches during the day. Orders were received that section of 2nd East Anglian Bde. were to go	

WAR DIARY or INTELLIGENCE SUMMARY

Army Form C. 2118.

Place	Date	Hour	Summary of Events and Information	Remarks and references to Appendices
VERMELLES	28/12/15 29/12/15		Our three sections were again relieved by our sections during the evening R/B. Enemy's Artillery again active on our (trenches). (Lt. R H Bingham proceeded on leave and WAR DIARY handed over to Lt A Butcher RTR.) R/B.	
	30/12/15		Until 4-20pm the day was very quiet, at that time the enemy exploded five mines round old line of the HAIRPIN (G.5.D.91. of Trench map Fontn: Sheet No 3, 36 c. N.W.) The 72nd Brigade RTR immediately opened a "barrage" along the German front line trenches, no attack followed the explosions and the situation quieted down again by 7-30 p.m., the rest of the day was quiet. (J.T.B Batchelor Lieut RTR)	
	31/12/15		Hostile Artillery was very active today and shelled the NOYELLES — LE SAULEHOY FARM roads and the NOYELLES — SAILLY LA BOURSE Road with 4.2" shells, the 72nd Brigade RTR retaliated on the Road H.I.6 extent to H.9.a extent (Trench Map Fontn: Ed. No 3, 36 c. NW) which had the desired effect, about 2 pm, the rest of the day was quiet. (J.T Batchelor Lieut RTR) J W Stirling Lt Colonel commanding 72nd Brigade RTR	X shown 36 B N E

72nd Bde: R.F.A.
Vol: 7
Jan '16

15th Div.

Army Form C. 2118.

WAR DIARY
or
INTELLIGENCE SUMMARY.
(Erase heading not required.)

Instructions regarding War Diaries and Intelligence Summaries are contained in F. S. Regs., Part II. and the Staff Manual respectively. Title pages will be prepared in manuscript.

Place	Date	Hour	Summary of Events and Information	Remarks and references to Appendices
Vermelles	1/7/16 2/7/16		Situation very quiet. Nothing of importance to report. Enemy trifling artillery action today and shelled our supports trenches between B.N.B.&P. and 8.11.B.25. (Ref. Trench Map 36a NW 3 Prov. Ed. No. 3) with 5.9" shells to which we retaliated with the support of an Heavy Howitzer Group.	AB
	3/7/16		Situation quiet & slow. Heavily fine & rain. Nothing of importance to report.	AB
	4/7/16		The infantry of the 47d. (London) Division were relieved that by the 2nd Durmouth (London) Division and the 42nd Brigade Rgt. came under their orders and supplied from 6 p.m. ___ AB	AB
	5/7/16		The day was very quiet, very clear and the aircraft of both sides were very active. During the day one gun of "D" Battery 42d Brigade R.F.A. was in action & fired 18 rounds.	AB
	6/7/16		One section of A, B, C and "D" Batteries 42d Bryts. R.F.A. proceeded back to Rue Rillues at CAVEHY-a-la-TOUR (Ref. Map HAZEBROUCK S.A. 1/100.000 B.F.)	AB

1577 Wt.W10791/1773 500,000 1/15 D. D. & L. A.D.S.S./Forms/C. 2118.

Army Form C. 2118.

WAR DIARY
or
INTELLIGENCE SUMMARY.

(Erase heading not required.)

Instructions regarding War Diaries and Intelligence Summaries are contained in F.S. Regs., Part II. and the Staff Manual respectively. Title pages will be prepared in manuscript.

Place	Date	Hour	Summary of Events and Information	Remarks and references to Appendices
FERMELLES	6/12 (cont.)		The Sections of "B" and "D" Batteries were relieved by "F" Battery R.H.A. and the N Normakolin Horse artillery Battery. Much of the VII Brigade R.H.A. division today very quiet.	A13
	7/12		The remaining sections of "A", "B" & "D" Batteries were relieved at 5-30 pm and proceeded to CAUCHY-a-la-TOUR into Billets and rejoined the 15th Divisional Artillery in Corps Reserve, the VII Brigade R.H.A took over the Sector hitherto held by 72nd Brigade R.G.A. from 6 pm on this day.	
			In A13 Corps Reserve ditto	A13
CAUCHY -a-la- Tour	8/12 9/12 10/12		Inspected by Major-General H.N.A. Melrotor L.B. D.S.O. Commanding XV Division who expressed his satisfaction at the appearance of the men and Horses of the Brigade after having been in action continuously for three weeks.	AR

1577 Wt. W10791/1773 500,000 1/15 D.D.&L. A.D.S.S./Forms/C. 2118.

WAR DIARY or INTELLIGENCE SUMMARY.

Army Form C. 2118.

Place	Date	Hour	Summary of Events and Information	Remarks and references to Appendices
CAUCHY	11/7/15		} In 4th Corps Reserve.	AAB
- do -	12/7/15			
TINQUES	13/7/15		In 4th Corps Reserve Battery Commanders went up to reconnoitre positions to be taken over.	AAB
"	14/7/15			
"	15/7/15		Still in 4th Corps Reserve. One section from each battery went up and took over from the following batteries:- 1 Section A/172 relieved 1 Section 114 Battery 1st Division. 1 Section B/172 relieved 1 Section 113 Battery. 1 Section D/172 relieved 1 Section 116 Battery 1st Division. e/172 taking over empty gun positions and 1 lone gun. AAB	
VERMELLES	16/7/15		Remainder of 172 Bde came up. H.Q. established in MAP 28 Fws Keep 9.15 B.4.4. Batteries carrying out Registration AAB	X: Ref H00000? 36c.N W/3. 1/10.000
"	17/7/15		Quiet Day. Batteries Registering. AAB. 24K K Tweed of C/172 wounded	
"	18/7/15		Quiet day. Registering continued AAB While observing in a front trench. AAB	
"	19/7/15		Quiet day. Registering Continued AAB	

WAR DIARY or INTELLIGENCE SUMMARY

Army Form C. 2118.

Place	Date	Hour	Summary of Events and Information	Remarks and references to Appendices
VERMELLES	19.1.16		The enemy shelled our trenches during the afternoon with 5.9" in G18C. All Batteries kept up a fire on their high lines, in connection is a view of the enemies at G.12.b.4.2.2 & G.12.b.4.2½ also MB 36c NW3.	Ref: 1/10000 hp 36c NW3.
	20.1.16		Quiet day. Fire was kept up on enemys trenches G.12.b.3.4½ to G.6.d.5½.0 and G.12.b.6.1 also G.12.b.8.1 to G.12.b.3.4½ to prevent in connection with mine. AB	Ref. Some AB map
	21.1.16		Quiet day. AB	
	22.1.16		During the morning and early afternoon the Batteries were heavily shelled with 4.2", 5.9" and 8" shells from HAISNES. Some material damage was done and one man wounded. No guns were damaged. AB	
	23.1.16		Quiet day. Carried out TEST ATTACK at 12.50pm. AB	
	24.1.16		Quiet day. AB	
	25.1.16		Quiet day. AB	
	26.1.16		Enemy shelled our trenches very heavily from about 8–9am in G.18 and G.17 B.c.d, we retaliated also slightly at 3pm in [R.c.e] we again retaliated. AB	Ref: Sewers up as above
	27.1.16		At 6.15am we fired an organised Bombardment on the German front line and communication trenches in H.13a H.13c H.7e.e D. G.12.B. (Ref. Sewer map as above.)	

1577 Wt.W10791/1773 500,000 1/15 D.D.&L. A.D.S.S./Forms/C. 2118.

Army Form C. 2118.

WAR DIARY
or
INTELLIGENCE SUMMARY.
(Erase heading not required.)

Place	Date	Hour	Summary of Events and Information	Remarks and references to Appendices
VERMELLES	25.1.15	(cont)	By orders from 15th I.A. At about 5.25pm the enemy were reported to be attacking on right, a Barrage was opened on the Enemy's lines in the same places as the above bombardment. All quiet after this during the night. A/B	X Atd
	26.1.15		Special Bombardment No. 24. aeroplanes A/72. Fixed H13.d.4.2.5 # B.a.2.6 B/72. H13.a.3.7.5 H.7.e.1.2. C/72 H.13.a.2.6. to H.7.e.1.2. D/72 H.13.a.4.7.5 H.7.e.4.8. & was repeated at 5.30pm and 9.45pm. (About) 7.20pm the enemy opened a heavy fire at 9.12 + 4.2½ at Batteries 72 B.A. concentrated on their fire. Nothing further to report. A.B.	
	29.1.15		Special Bombardment No 25. aeroplanes A/72 C.Trench H.19.d.2.4.2.7. C.Trench from H.1.b.2.3. C.Trench H.19.d.2.7.7. — 4.2.3. Bn Hqa.6.5- H.13.c.5 o C/72 H.19.b.2.4. H.13.c.8.2. C.Trench from H.13.c.B.2. C.Trench from H.13.c.8.2. Bgn carried out at 7am repeated 4.55pm 6.16pm. Quiet day. A.B.	
	30.1.15		Quiet day. A.B.	
	31.1.15		The enemy shelled our support lines in 9.16.6. slightly otherwise all quiet. A.B.	

J. McStirling
Colonel 92. Mid R.F.A.

2/16

WAR DIARY
INTELLIGENCE SUMMARY

Army Form C. 2118.

Place	Date	Hour	Summary of Events and Information	Remarks and references to Appendices
MERVILLE	31.1.16		List of names of Officers and other Ranks mentioned in despatches of 1.1.16 and Honours in the Gazette 18.1.16	

MENTIONED IN DESPATCHES.

Colonel J. W. Stirling RFA Commanding 72 Bde RFA
Major A.W.T. Elaen RFA Commanding C.172 Bde RFA
C/Lieut A.T.G. Gardner RFA Commanding B/172 Bde RFA
Lt. R.H. Bingham RFA
2F/A W. Grout RFA "A/172 Bde RFA
No. Bomb J. Gray B/172 Bde RFA

HONOURS.
Officers. Lt. R.H. Bingham. Military Cross.
O.Ranks. No Bomb R. J. Gray. D.C.M.

Brigadier H.A. Wilkin. Interpreter 72 Bde RFA. D.C.M.

J. W. Stirling
Colonel 72 B-R-F-A

2/2/16

72nd Bde: R7a.
Vol: 8

(15)

WAR DIARY
INTELLIGENCE SUMMARY

Army Form C. 2118.

Place	Date	Hour	Summary of Events and Information	Remarks and references to Appendices
VERMELLES	1/7/16		Quiet day. RAB	
	2/7/16		Retaliation for ??? on our trenches. A little shorts of our registration done RAB	
	3/7/16		Quiet day. At about 5.50 put up barrage on night lines for reported gas attack on our right. RAB	
	4/7/16		Quiet day. RAB	
	5/7/16		Carried our 3 special Bombardments [Frightfulness No 26] at 2pm 3.45pm 11 minutes all quiet. RAB	
	6/7/16		Quiet day. Lt J.W. Stirling proceeded on leave. Maj J.W. Saville took command of the Brigade. A/172 was heavily shelled during the morning and afternoon. No damage done. RAB	
	7/7/16		Some aeroplane registration done otherwise all quiet. RAB	
	8/7/16		A few (pile Saucake) light field gun fire on our trenches was retaliated on. RAB	
	9/7/16		Quiet day. 9 rds 5.9 shells on A/172. 2 Lt J F Dyer wounded. RAB	
	10/7/16		No enemy fired a good deal with 4.2" shells on our trenches today not retaliated. RAB	

Army Form C. 2118.

Instructions regarding War Diaries and Intelligence Summaries are contained in F. S. Regs., Part II. and the Staff Manual respectively. Title pages will be prepared in manuscript.

WAR DIARY
or
INTELLIGENCE SUMMARY.
(Erase heading not required.)

Place	Date	Hour	Summary of Events and Information	Remarks and references to Appendices
VERMELLES	11/2/16		Slight enemy activity against our trenches during the morning. At about 5 pm the enemy flew a mine in front of our trenches in H.13.c* All Batteries concentrated with Enemy front line and communication trenches in this area. AAA3	*Ref. 110000 Trench Map 36c NW Edition 6. AAA3
	12/2/16		Enemy shelled our trenches heavily in G.3.d* and P.2.d.f* during the later part of the morning and in the afternoon this became quite intense between 3.30 - 5.30pm. Our Batteries retaliated. AAA3	*Ref. Trench Map 36c NW Edition 6. AAA3
	13/2/16		Quiet day. A few rifle grenades on our front line in P.2.d. S/17x fired on enemy trenches and stopped this. AAA3	
	14/2/16		Quiet day. Nothing to report. AAA3	
	15/2/16		A few Rapnipe light field gun shells on our trenches in G.12.d* were fired during the e/17x retaliated on Enemy's front line & Batteries with effect. AAA3	*As above AAA3
	16/2/16		Very quiet day. Nothing to report. AAA3	
	17/2/16		Batteries carried out Special Bombardment of Road in G.31.c & B.1.6 at AAA3. Col J.W.B. Loring left 72Bde RFA. Hon. Leuy Gen. L. Lowe in issue. AAA3	

Army Form C. 2118.

WAR DIARY
or
INTELLIGENCE SUMMARY.
(Erase heading not required.)

Instructions regarding War Diaries and Intelligence Summaries are contained in F. S. Regs., Part II. and the Staff Manual respectively. Title pages will be prepared in manuscript.

Place	Date	Hour	Summary of Events and Information	Remarks and references to Appendices
VERMELLES	18/7/16	4.5.45am	Batteries carried out a Bombardment of the German Road in C.17a & C.17.15. Quiet during the day. The usual going round to N15 rights 11.45PM was ordered by 15th D.A. the Colot fire 5pm - 11.15pm. PAB	
	19/7/16		Quiet day. PAB	
	20/7/16		B Battery 72"Bde was shelled today between 1pm - 2.15pm and 5 - 9 Wells landed. Hit on a dug out no damage done. PAB	
	21/7/16		Quiet day. All Batteries took part in Bombardment of the German Line Craters at H.13.c 4.7 and H.14.c 4.9 in conjunction with the Russels between 2.30pm and 3.15pm. at 5.15pm B/72 and C/72 fired on main Road running through HULLUCH. PAB	K(?) H.20.a Ph(?) R.M.C.H begin 143 Extn. G. ditto
	22/7/16		A few light shells on our front line in G.2.D and H.13.C at 9pm and 5pm otherwise all quiet. All Batteries fired on works in front of (Pub) 13 tr's a 7pm and (5.16am 23/7/16). C/72 fired with other transport head in HULLUCH during the evening. PAB	ditto
	23/7/16	12.15am	repeated fire on main Road in HULLUCH with B/72 & C/72. Very Quiet during the day. PAB	
	24/7/16		Very quiet day. PAB	

Army Form C. 2118.

WAR DIARY
or
INTELLIGENCE SUMMARY.
(Erase heading not required.)

Instructions regarding War Diaries and Intelligence Summaries are contained in F. S. Regs., Part II. and the Staff Manual respectively. Title pages will be prepared in manuscript.

Place	Date	Hour	Summary of Events and Information	Remarks and references to Appendices
VERMELLES	25/2/16		Quiet day. Heavy snow. We flew a mine at about H13a2.1 ell Battn's of 72 Bde put up a barrage along German front line. Communication trenches and 2 mine deposits the vicinity of our mine. PAA3.	Ref. 1000 map Trenches 36cNW1 Edn. 6
	26/2/16		Hostile trench mortar activity against our front line in H13c, H13a, G18b, or about 5.30 pm. this was silenced by fire from A/72 and B/72. PAA3	ditto
	27/2/16		Very quiet day. PAA3.	
	28/2/16		Quiet day. A few rifle grenades on our front line in G18e C/72 retaliated PAA3	
	29/2/16		Quiet day. Nothing to report	

J. W. Sterling
Colonel Commanding
72 PAB

3/2/16

Confidential   A.B/19.

2nd April 1916

D.A.G. "at" the Base
———————————

        Herewith War Diary completed for the month of March 1916 forwarded for retention please.

                     A Butcher
                     Lieut. for
                     Colonel R.J.R.
       Commanding 72nd Bde R.J.R.

72 RFA
Vol 9

WAR DIARY
or
INTELLIGENCE SUMMARY
(Erase heading not required.)

Army Form C. 2118.

Place	Date	Hour	Summary of Events and Information	Remarks and references to Appendices
VERMELLES	1/3/16		A quiet day. Some registration closely by all batteries a little field gun pro on our front line during the afternoon. RAB	
	2/3/16		Enemy shelled our support trench's heavily between 4 pm and 5 pm. Nothing further to report. RAB	
	3/3/16		At 6 pm and 6.55 pm A172 B/72 C/72 Bombarded the German rest & Hulloch Belgian corner & 8/172 swept. The enemy shelled VERMELLES heavily, unk 5.9" shells 6 pm and 7 pm the enemy put up a great amount of work at about 8.30 pm. All batteries opened fire on their night lines. RAB	
	4/3/16		Between 6-7 am enemy shelled VERMELLES trench with 5.9" shells. One gunner B/172 slightly wounded. 1 man of D/172 killed again in the evening C/172 + D/172 were shelled with 5.9" shells from direction of Douvrin. No damage done. RAB	
	5/3/16		Quiet day. D/172 did some hostile fire registration. RAB	
	6/3/16		Enemy shelled our reserve trenches in H.13 a.b.c wire during the afternoon. B/172 retaliated. C/72 did a special shoot to try and lift French batteries fire 72 rounds on German front line in H.13 a. The was also return fire.	
	7/3/16		Very quiet day.	

WAR DIARY
or
INTELLIGENCE SUMMARY.

(Erase heading not required.)

Army Form C. 2118.

Place	Date	Hour	Summary of Events and Information	Remarks and references to Appendices
VERMELLES	8/3/16		During the evening between 10.30 and 11am A17z and B17z were shelled with 5.9" and 4.2" from Loos and Wingles. Our little material damage was done was soon repaired. No casualties. The enemy shelled Spoon Lane with 5.9" D17z retaliated. R+B	
	9/3/16		The enemy billeted our front line in H13c with rifle grenades D17z was successful in stopping this by gun-cop. The German front line in H13c & R+B	⅔ Rg 1/10000 Map Sht 36 ⅓
	10/3/16		Quiet day nothing to report	
	11/3/16		Early in the afternoon the enemy shelled our trenches with 5.9" shells in G12R otherwise quiet day. R+B	
	12/3/16		The enemy shelled our support and communication trenches all the afternoon with 5.9" and 77 guns. Shells in G18 we retaliated on enemy 2nd line trails and on Hulluch. C17z retaliated during the night for rifle Grenades on our front line in H13 c D17z at 9pm fired on enemy transport on the Haisnes road in Hulluch R+B	
	13/3/16		Enemy shelled our support line in G12 B with 5.9" during the afternoon. Otherwise quiet. R+B	

WAR DIARY
or
INTELLIGENCE SUMMARY.
(Erase heading not required.)

Army Form C. 2118.

Place	Date	Hour	Summary of Events and Information	Remarks and references to Appendices
RICHEBG	14/3/16		At 2 noon today the 12th Division on our left took over the defence of front our line down as far South as STONESTREET. 72 R.d. Bde is now responsible for the defence of the line Zones marked on German front line H19a.8.2 - A17c.9.1. Quiet day nothing to report. PAB	
"	15/3/16		Quiet day. Battn's registering. PAB	
"	16/3/16		Very little was heavily shelled today with 5.9" no damage done in the Brigade	
"	17/3/16		The enemy shelled our trenches in H19a fairly heavily during the morning. A17z retaliated 9 to 10 a.m. 6/17z A.A. combined shoot with trenches on enemy line opposite Northern and Southern Saps. H13.c. D17z knocked out a snipers post at H13.a.7.8. Hostile A/llery was active on our trench most of the day. PAB At H.H.10a.m. (PP.1) having been attacked for 10 Stocks to A17z since 3.3.16 left today for England. PAB	
"	18/3/16		A little enemy artillery fire on our trenches in H13.c. during the morning. In the evening about 5.30 p.m. - 7 p.m. the enemy shelled trenches and Battery positions with salvo & rapid fire of guns and howitzers also put up a barrage of gas shells that developed into an attack a bit to	

WAR DIARY or INTELLIGENCE SUMMARY

Army Form C. 2118.

Place	Date	Hour	Summary of Events and Information	Remarks and references to Appendices
KEMMEL	18/7/16		work in progress against 12th Division. We form a supporting barrage on enemy's southern flank in support of 12th Division.	
	19/7/16		A little shelling of our support line in Sqr. B.17.2. retaliated. One section of 16th Division Artillery A.182 arrived today to be attached to B/172 for instruction. Lt Short arrived to be attached to 72 Bde H.Q. R.A.	
	20/7/16		Intermittent shelling of communication trenches in Sq.9a.b. during the morning. Shrapnel & trench mortar R.A.B.	
	21/7/16		Hun shells on our communication trenches during the day. Answer in quiet R.A.B. Lt. M. Smith 2/3 Medium R.F.A. attached to B/172 for Instruction. Bde Support R.A.B.	
	22/7/16		Quiet day. Nothing to report. R.A.B.	
	23/7/16		Hostile Artillery active against our reserve trenches in 9.3.a & 3. Nothing further to report. R.A.B.	
	24/7/16		Quiet day. At 10.30 mn Test Attack was sent out from 1st D.A. H.Q. all Batteries had fired within 3 minutes of message being received w/Bde H.Q.	

WAR DIARY
or
INTELLIGENCE SUMMARY.

Army Form C. 2118.

Place	Date	Hour	Summary of Events and Information	Remarks and references to Appendices
VERMELLES	25th		All quiet nothing to Report.	
	26th		Quiet during the day. The Infantry of the VII Division was Relieved by the Infantry of the XVI Division during afternoon and evening. Before the relief was complete the enemy blew up about C/13c.4.7.2. about 60 yds of trench was blown in. B/172 C/172 and 1/K3 Coy N3 D/172 opened fire on enemy trenches opposite C/172. D/172 carried on with the foregoing all night. Saved opening fault's. The Sections of 161 Inf Bty attached 67?BdE were changed today. The night & postn? R/H.B without further without incident	FA 6
	27/7/15		A few shells on our supply trenches during the day M/13	
	28/7/15 29/7/15 30/7/15 31/7/15		Nothing of importance to report.	

Wm Stirling Colonel R.F.A.
Commanding 42nd Bde R.F.A.

72 RFA
Vol 10

Army Form C. 2118.

WAR DIARY
or
INTELLIGENCE SUMMARY.
(Erase heading not required.)

Instructions regarding War Diaries and Intelligence Summaries are contained in F. S. Regs., Part II. and the Staff Manual respectively. Title pages will be prepared in manuscript.

Place	Date	Hour	Summary of Events and Information	Remarks and references to Appendices
VERMELLES	1/7/16	10pm	45th Inf Bde successfully exploded a mine at H.13.A.21. (Trench Map 36cNW Sheet 6.) 'B', 'C' + 'D' batteries supported the explosion.	
—do—	2/7/16	10pm	Quiet day, nothing to report	
—do—	3/7/16	—	Sections of C/182 and D/182 Brigade RFA reported 16th Divl Artillery. Situation quiet.	
—do—	4/7/16	4.35pm	Mine successfully exploded at end of SOUTHERN SAP, H.13.c.4.9½ (Trench Map 36cNW) C/72 + supported the explosion and 'B' + 'C' Batteries fired in retaliation to enemy's Rifle grenades and trench mortars.	
—do—	5/7/16	—	Situation quiet, nothing to report.	
—do—	6/7/16	—	Enemy bombarded our front and support lines with 5.9s and 4.2s in H.19.A (Trench Map 36cNW) under heavy between 12.30pm + 2.45pm	
—do—	7/7/16	—	Situation quiet, nothing to report	
—do—	8/7/16	—	ditto	
—do—	9/7/16	—	ditto	
—do—	10/7/16	—	ditto	

Army Form C. 2118

WAR DIARY
or
INTELLIGENCE SUMMARY

(Erase heading not required.)

Instructions regarding War Diaries and Intelligence Summaries are contained in F. S. Regs., Part II. and the Staff Manual respectively. Title Pages will be prepared in manuscript.

Place	Date	Hour	Summary of Events and Information	Remarks and references to Appendices
VERMELLES.	11/4/16		Enemy fired a few Rifle Grenades on our front line during the afternoon.	PAB.
	12/4/16		Support Reserve and Communication Trenches in Hulluch Sector Shelled with 4.2" and 77mm (Pipsqueaks) all the afternoon. We retaliated.	PAB.
	13/4/16		Quiet day. A/172 and D/172 relieved in the line by A/182 & D/182. 16th Division Batteries of 72nd Bde went back into Reserve.	PAB.
	14/4/16		Situation very quiet. Nothing to report.	PAB.
	15/4/16		All quiet nothing to report.	PAB.
	16/4/16		At 2.a.m. the enemy made a small bombing attack on the crater at H13c 2.9. C/172 fired in support of the infantry. C/172 & B/172 and H.Q. relieved in the line by C/182. B/182. and A.Q. 181/Bde RFA. Brigade went into rest in billets at BELLERY.	PAB
BELLERY.	17/4/16		Bde in G.H.Q. reserve at BELLERY.	PAB
	18/4/16		do	PAB.
	19/4/16		do	PAB.

WAR DIARY
~~INTELLIGENCE SUMMARY~~

(Erase heading not required.)

Army Form C. 2118

Place	Date	Hour	Summary of Events and Information	Remarks and references to Appendices
FLECHIN	20/4/16		Bde. moved to Special Training area in good billets as follows. A/72 BONCOUR. B/72. FLECHIN C/72. PIPEMONT. D/72 FLECHIN Bde Hd.Qrs FLECHIN PM3	
"	21/4/16		do PM3	
"	22/4/16		do PM3	
"	23/4/16		Easter Sy. Batteries continue to do training under Battery Commanders. PM3	
BELLERY	24/4/16		Tactical Exercise for the whole Brigade during the day. returned to Battery at about 7pm. Same day. PM3	
	25/4/16		Bde in billets at BELLERY PM3.	
	26/4/16		do PM3	
	27/4/16		do PM3. At 7 am orders were received for 72nd Brigade to "Stand to" in order to move up to the front under a defence Scheme. as the Enemy were making a gas attack. This order cancelled at 12 noon. PM3.	
	28/4/16		First half of 72 Bde moved up into the line in relief of 12" Division Artillery. 62nd Bde.	

Army Form C. 2118

WAR DIARY
or
INTELLIGENCE SUMMARY
(*Erase heading not required.*)

Instructions regarding War Diaries and Intelligence
Summaries are contained in F. S. Regs., Part II.
and the Staff Manual respectively. Title Pages
will be prepared in manuscript.

Place	Date	Hour	Summary of Events and Information	Remarks and references to Appendices
VERQUIGNEUL	29/4/16		Second half of Brigade AB arrived up into the line in relief of 12" D.A. 62nd Bde RFA. Bde HQ remain at VERQUIGNEUL. Batteries from part of Rifler Group. Under Lt-Col CHRISTIE. RFA. A&B	
	30/4/16		Nothing to report.	

1 5/16

M Bucket
Lieut for
Blane. RFA.
Commanding 72nd Bde RFA.

72.R.F.A.
Vol. 11
Army Form C. 2118

WAR DIARY
or
INTELLIGENCE SUMMARY
(Erase heading not required.)

Place	Date	Hour	Summary of Events and Information	Remarks and references to Appendices
VERQUIGNEUL	1/5/15 to 21/5/16	—	Nothing to report. "A" "B" "C" and "D" Batteries under the Right Group XVth Divisional Artillery	A13
"	22/5/16	—	72nd Bde R.F.A. Ammunition Column reorganised and formed into No. 3 Section 15th Divisional Ammunition Column. Captain R.E. Reed R.F.A., 7/horse C.A. Bowles, 7/horse C. Mead, 139 N.C.Os and men, 16 Riding and 135 Heavy Draught, and 12 mules transferred to 15th D.A.C.	A13
"	9/5/16	—	Major the Lord Wynford R.F.A. promoted Lieut-Colonel and posted to Command 45th Divisional Artillery (1/1st South Midland Brigade R.F.A. (T.F.)).	A13
"	19/5/16	—	Captain F. Graham R.J.O. R.F.A. joined the Brigade and assumed Command of D/72nd Brigade R.F.A.	A13
"	20/5/16 to 31/5/16	—	Nothing to Report. A B C & D Batteries Still under Right Group 15th Divisional Artillery.	

PAB PABingham
for Colonel, R.F.A.
Commanding 72nd Brigade R.F.A.

June
Army Form C. 2118

WAR DIARY or INTELLIGENCE SUMMARY
(Erase heading not required.)

72 RFA XV VOL

Place	Date	Hour	Summary of Events and Information	Remarks and references to Appendices
VERQUIGNEUL.	1.6/16 to 4.6/16		Batteries of 72 Bde. in action under Right Group of D.A. Quiet day.	RAB.
VERMELLES.	5.6/16		Col. J. W. Stirling takes over command of Right Group of Divisional Artillery. Quiet day.	RAB.
	6.6/16 7.6/16		A few working parties seen and dispersed. Hostile Artillery quiet. Reorganisation of Batteries in 15 Div took place. D/172. Howitzer Battery commanded by Maj Settimus. New D/172. 4.5 Howitzer Battery commanded by Maj Settimus. 15 Div Artillery. Quiet day.	RAB.
	8.6/16.		CORONS. DE RUTOIRE were heavily shelled during the day. We flew a mine at about G.11.B.3.5. at 8.pm enemy shelled our trenches from about 8.15pm to 9.15 in G.11.B. not retaliated.	RAB.
	9.6/16 10.6/16		Quiet day. Hostile Artillery shelled our trenches in H.19a. a little a two working parties were seen and dispersed.	RAB.
	11.6/16 12.6/16		Nothing to Report. RAB. Batteries D/170 Div Artillery relieved by Batteries of 40th Div Artillery. C/185. in Right Group for instruction. Batteries of the Group registered the German wire along their front. RAB.
	13.6/16		Quiet day. Enemy shelled VENDIN. ALLEY. for about 20 minutes with 4.2" RAB.
	14.6/16		Enemy shelled VENDIN. ALLEY. and our trenches in H.19a. Several times during the day. Hostile working parties were dispersed. RAB.
	15.6/16		Enemy shelled our trenches in G.12c at 4.30pm and 6pm. RAB.

Army Form C. 2118

WAR DIARY
or
INTELLIGENCE SUMMARY

(Erase heading not required.)

Instructions regarding War Diaries and Intelligence Summaries are contained in F. S. Regs., Part II. and the Staff Manual respectively. Title Pages will be prepared in manuscript.

Place	Date	Hour	Summary of Events and Information	Remarks and references to Appendices
VERMELLES	16/6/16		Hostile Artillery very active against our trenches in G.2.c. all day. enemy were also using heavy trench mortars against trench at the same time. We retaliated. RAB.	
	17/6/16		Very quiet day. RAB.	
	18/6/16		Hostile artillery very active against our trenches in G.11.B and G.11.D. G11e was also heavily shelled. We retaliated each time. Between 3.30 and 4pm A172 and A170 in position in G.11.B. were heavily shelled with A.2 and 5.9" from the direction of Twingies. RAB	
	19/6/16		Quiet day. Nothing to report. RAB	
	20/6/16		Quiet day. RAB	
	21/6/16		Quiet day. RAB	
	22/6/16		Hostile Artillery fairly active during the evening. A stray 9.am. of our Vickers aeroplanes was brought down in the enemy lines, from W. of Auchy.	
	23/6/16		Hostile Artillery Active. Heavy working parties engaged opposite Hulluch section.	

WAR DIARY or INTELLIGENCE SUMMARY

Army Form C. 2118

Place	Date	Hour	Summary of Events and Information	Remarks and references to Appendices
VERMELLES	24/6/16		Special offensive operations against the enemy on the whole of the 2" Div front by daily and nightly forward moves. Gas and smoke, clouds and raids. Operations mentioned in this diary relate only to the Horwich sector. That is opposite the front. 9u.B.7.4. to H.19.A.33. * Today is M day. Snipers posts and M.G.emplacements engaged. Tracks communication (Trawler and Trench Railways) fired on during the night. To H. Retaliation very slight.	1/Rl Irish. King 36thInf WS. Col 6
	25/6/16		2nd Day. Same as M day.	
	26/6/16		3rd Day. Wire cutting at 9.12 & 58. and same as M day. 44th Infantry Bde carried out a raid at 9.12.=8. Wire was cut by Cap. M.Y. Garner. B.72 RFA. PAB	
	27/6/16		4th Day. Same as M day. and ordinary shelling of enemy's communications at night at 1.10 am. 2.40 am. L.W. was sent over outs whole front. Raiding parties went out after the L.W. at H.30.5.3.1. and 2 points south to and within 200 yds of this point without much success. Artillery arrangements was cut by Maj Kidd RFA A70 and so a fine further north by Capt Treasty A.7.2.	
	28/6/16		5th Day. Same as M day, and night. PAB	

1875 Wt. W593/826 1,000,000 4/15 T.R.C. & A. A.D.S.S./Forms/C. 2118.

Army Form C. 2118

WAR DIARY
or
INTELLIGENCE SUMMARY

(Erase heading not required.)

Instructions regarding War Diaries and Intelligence
Summaries are contained in F. S. Regs., Part II.
and the Staff Manual respectively. Title Pages
will be prepared in manuscript.

Place	Date	Hour	Summary of Events and Information	Remarks and references to Appendices
VERMELLES.	29/9/16		6th day. Same as 1st day. Puits 13 Bis was bombarded by 4.5 Hows. 4.5" J.B. conducted a raid on the enemy Trenches at the HOHENZOLLERN. PtB	*Since posted to C Battery 71 Bde RFA.
	30/9/16		7th day. Quiet day all forms restricted to retaliation only. PtB	
			Honours and Rewards during the Month – 72 Bde RFA.	
			(MENTIONED) IN DESPATCHES 3 June 1916. Col. J. W. Stirling RFA	
			*Lt. J. C. RUSSELL. RFA	
			MILITARY CROSS.	

J. W. Stirling Col. RFA.

Comg. 72nd Bde. RFA.

WAR DIARY
INTELLIGENCE SUMMARY

(Erase heading not required.)

Army Form C. 2118

1st July
72 RFA

Place	Date	Hour	Summary of Events and Information	Remarks and references to Appendices
VERMELLES	1.7/16		8th Day of Special Offensive. This consisted of concentrated retaliation on certain fixed points during the day and firing on enemy's communications during the night. PMB	Vol
	2.7/16		9th Day of Special Offensive B72 and A70 cut wire during the day. At 10.15pm all Batteries fired in support for a small raid. PMB	
	3.7/16		10th Day. Retaliation carried out. A good many working parties were engaged and dispersed. The Strontzers fired on enemy M.G. emplacements. PMB	
	4.7/16		B72 cut wire at 9.2.B.9.6 as a blind. At 11.5pm the 46th SRH carried out a successful raid on the German trenches opposite HULLOCH. R. wire had been previously cut by our Capt Gardner B72 was were as mentioned further with as a blind. RA arrangements worked well. Both of the Artillery and the Infantry from 13 B.20 I.R. enemy were killed and we took 2 prisoners, who belonged to V Bavarian Regt. I Bavarian Corps. The remainder of the night passed off quietly. PMB	
	5.7/16		11th Day. Programme day again consisted of Retaliation. Enemy working parties were again engaged and dispersed. At 11.30pm gas was sent over again along the whole front. We bombarded a certain places. PMB	

Army Form C. 2118

WAR DIARY
or
INTELLIGENCE SUMMARY
(Erase heading not required.)

Instructions regarding War Diaries and Intelligence Summaries are contained in F. S. Regs., Part II. and the Staff Manual respectively. Title Pages will be prepared in manuscript.

Place	Date	Hour	Summary of Events and Information	Remarks and references to Appendices
VERMELLES	6.7.16		Lt. Ingram. RFA. 73rd R.A. RFA. took over command of Right Gp. of S.A. from Lt. Gun Stirling RFA Comy 72 Bde RFA. 72 Bde Gp. came back to BETHUNE	PAB
BETHUNE	7.7.16 to 16.7.16		Nothing to report.	PAB
"			- - moved to VERQUIGNEUL	PAB
VERQUIGNEUL	17.7.16 to 18.7.16		Nothing to Report.	PAB
"	18.7.16		Lt L. F. S. Baen. B7x. Wounded. 2 other ranks gassed. Nothing further to report	PAB Ref. 11000000 map LENS.
"	19.7.16 to 22.7.16		Nothing to Report	PAB
"	22.7.16 to 23.7.16		" " RFA.	PAB
"	24.7.16		½ 72nd Bde moved into Concentration Area. at BERGUINEUSE Remaining half 72 Bde RFA moved to BERGUINEUSE. Lt. V. H. Mead was killed whilst in the trenches and was buried in VERMELLES.	PAB
BERGUINEUSE FILLIEVRES.	25.7.16 → 26.7.16		Quiet day. Nothing to report 72 Bde marched from BERGUINEUSE to FILLIEVRES a distance under orders from H Q DA about 15 miles. following under orders of Batteries, H.Q. Staff. D.C.B.A.	PAB
MEZEROLLES	27.7.16		72 Bde marched from FILLIEVRES to MEZEROLLES, under orders from H. S.A. in the following under H.Q. Staff A.E.D.B. distance about 13 miles. Suspected on the march by C.R.A. MDiv	PAB

1875 Wt. W 593/826 1,000,000 4/15 J.B.C. & A. A.D.S.S./Forms/C. 2118.

Army Form C. 2118

WAR DIARY
or
INTELLIGENCE SUMMARY
(Erase heading not required.)

Instructions regarding War Diaries and Intelligence Summaries are contained in F. S. Regs., Part II. and the Staff Manual respectively. Title Pages will be prepared in manuscript.

Place	Date	Hour	Summary of Events and Information	Remarks and references to Appendices
HEM.	28.7.16		72nd Bde marched from MEZEROLLES to HEM under orders of the following order. H.Q. Staff A.C.D.B. inspected on the march by G.O.C. of Div. Arrived here about 12 noon. Excellent watering for the horses, distance about 12 miles up to the present there have been no casualties to men or horses during the 6 days march. R.M.B.	Reference Moreuil map. L.T.M.S.
"	29.7.16		Remained at HEM.	
"	30.7.16		2nd Lt. de VILLIERS joined the Bde for 2 days attached to report R.M.B. and rejoins proceed to B.70.	
BOURDON.	31.7.16		72nd Bde marched from HEM. to BOURDON under orders of the following order. H.Q. Staff. C.B. D.A. distance about 20 miles. Weather extremely hot. Arrived BOURDON at about 2 p.m. R.M.B.	" AMIENS.

31.7.16
BOURDON

J. W. Stirling
Colonel RFA
Commanding 72 Bde RFA.

15th Divisional Artillery.

72nd BRIGADE

ROYAL FIELD ARTILLERY

AUGUST 1 9 1 6

CONFIDENTIAL.

War Diary

72 Bde RFA

From 1st to 31st July, 1916.

E Boyce

1st August, 1916.   Major, R.A.
Bde Major, 15th Divnl. Arty.

CONFIDENTIAL.

WAR DIARY.

of

72nd Brigade R. F. A.

From 1st August, 1916   to   31st August, 1916.

VOLUME Number 13.

[signature]

Major, R.A.

Brigade Major R.A., 15th Divisional Artillery.

Confidential

To Headquarters
15th Divl Arty

Herewith War Diary for the month of July 1916.
Duplicate has been forwarded to Record Office

J. M. Sterling
Col. R.F.A.
Comdg 72nd Bde R.F.A.

31/7/16

To Headquarters   Confidential
   15th Div Arty

   Herewith War Diary for month of
August 1916.
   Duplicate has been forwarded to
Records

                    [signature]
                         Colonel, R.?.?
              Commanding 72nd Brigade, R.?.?

1916

Army Form C. 2118

15
72. R.F.A.
VOR14

WAR DIARY
or
INTELLIGENCE SUMMARY
(Erase heading not required.)

Place	Date	Hour	Summary of Events and Information	Remarks and references to Appendices
BOURDON.	1.8.16.		72nd Bde. Remained here for a day. Received orders to be prepared to move tomorrow. PAB	Ref. MAPS. LENS and AMIENS. 1/100000
BEHENCOURT.	2.8.16		The 72 Bde. marched from BOURDON to BEHENCOURT. Stay under orders from XIII DA. Weather extremely hot. No casualties to guns or horses.	
"	3.8.16		Orders received that 15th DA. to relieve 19 DA. in the line. I Section from each battery 72 Bde. went up and took over from its corresponding section in 88 Bde RFA XIX Div.	?
S23B 4.7.	4.8.16.		The remainder of 72nd Bde. moved up and took over from 88th Bde. 19th Div. Position. J.H.Q. and 3 Batteries (A.B.D./72) in S3 B.4.7. about 700 yds S.W. of BEZANTIN LE GRAND. wood. and 1 Battery C/72 in MAMETZ WOOD. Quiet after front. H.Q. and A.B.D. Batteries shelled with 4.2 and 77m shrapnel during the day and night. C/72 shelled with 5.9s. PAB.	?
"	5.8.16		Hostile Artillery active during the afternoon on our trenches in S3c and D. Batteries and H.Q. shelled during the night with 4.2" PAB	
"	6.8.16		H.Q. and A.B.D Batteries heavily shelled during the evening and all night with 4.2" 5.9s and 77mm shrapnel. PAB. Nothing to report.	
"	7.8.16		S20c. centrale was again heavily shelled. PAB. PAB	
"	8.8.16			
"	9.8.16			
"	10.8.16.		A/g. 72 Bde. by orders 15th JA. moved took to a position just north of the village of MAMETZ. a quiet day for battery positions in S20 c. C/72 fully shelled during the day. also our trenches in S3c and D. PAB M. Batteries supported an infantry attack during the night. PAB	
"	11.8.16		Nothing to Report. PAB	
"	12.8.16		Quiet during the day. During the night the 112th Infantry Bde. also carried out the North Australians and 15th Divs carried out an attack a small operation supported by their artillery and 15th DArtillery. All Batteries 72nd Bde. took part. PAB	

WAR DIARY or INTELLIGENCE SUMMARY

Army Form C. 2118

Place	Date	Hour	Summary of Events and Information	Remarks and references to Appendices
MAMETZ	13.8.16		72"Bde in conjunction with rest of 15"DA supported an attack by 112"Infantry Bde. In the early hours of the morning C/72 was heavily shelled. Lt. V. R. Barron slightly wounded. 3 men killed, 5 wounded, and 1 ammunition wagon destroyed. Also D/72 had a Sergeant killed. PMB	C.Battery in action N.10 corner of MAMETZ. WOOD
	14.8.16		C/72 moved our their positions and began taking in our right of D/72. About mid day the Batteries were heavily shelled for about half an hour with 5·9s and 4·2. Capt W.H.B. Saville, RFA was killed and two men wounded. The remainder of the day passed off smoothly. The 30th Div Infantry were relieved by 2nd Div Infantry who are now supporting. PMB	
	15.8.16		Quiet day on the whole. Batteries kept up an evolution barrage all day and night. PMB	
	16.8.16		At 7.15pm all Batteries helped in barrage on German advanced Trench in S3c and d in support of 2nd) Brigade attack which was successful. PMB	
	17.8.16		The Batteries of 72"Bde RFA where shelled during the morning with 5·9s Batteries kept up its Isolation Barrage in S3 b and d all day and night in preparation for an attack on the 18th inst. PMB	
	18.8.16		The Isolation Barrage was kept up during the morning. At 2.45pm the 2nd Division Infantry 2nd Infantry Bde in conjunction with 33 Div on the Right centred our an attack on High Wood and German trench in S2c. A.B and D/72 helped to create own Barrage in front of the assaulting infantry (2nd & 1B). Zero Time at 2.45pm. Left of A 70.3 yds enemies 200 yds. The 1st Div attack was a Success. Artillery arrangements apparently worked well. A few casualties today. Total up to date of Officers. 1 killed 1 wounded. PMB O.R. 4 " 16 "	

1875 Wt. W 593/826 1,000,000 4/15 J.B.C.&A. A.D.S.S./Forms/C. 2118.

WAR DIARY
INTELLIGENCE SUMMARY
(Erase heading not required.)

Army Form C. 2118

Place	Date	Hour	Summary of Events and Information	Remarks and references to Appendices
MAMETZ	19.8.16		The Enemy seemed to be very confused in our area. Batteries shelled switch line between M33 d50½ - M33d 2.1. Enemy artillery very quiet. The Batterie were not shelled. 2 men were wounded by prematures.	Ref LoqueME 11/9000 map
"	20.8.16		The situation is still rather involved. Quiet morning. The Batteries remained on the line M33 d 50½ - M33d 2.1. Switch line. The Batteries barraged on the line M33 d 50½ - M33d 2.1. and at 1.30pm 18pdr Bty Gp. Infantry again attacked the onto the Sunken road in M33 b. and we were able to fire about 300yds South of Switch line. The attack was wt quite a success corner of High wood and were repulsed. The enemy counter-attacked N.W. this eveng till about 2 am. At 10pm the Batteries were shelled heavily with gas shells.	A telegram of congratulation were wt musd 6th Div from G.O.C. 4th ARMY.
"	21.8.16		at 5 P.M. The enemy reported to be counter-attacking in High Wood. Casualty Officer slightly wound. M33 d 5.0 - M33d 0.7 D72 fired on Sunken road behind (NE) High Wood. A72 and B72 fired from This attack came to nothing ceased firing at 6 am. At 6 am C72 searched North of High Wood again. We a small barrage on Sunken Rd in Support during the morning. At 2.45pm our a telegram of Congrats received Our Infantry attack on Corr High Wr and left by 14th and 15 Corps. quiet day in the Battery positions. of 5½ Div. by 7 2 C in C. RHB shelled	C72 in action
"	22.8.16		Batteries were shelled from 8.30 pm Our trenches in S3 Quarry shelled. to 9pm with 5.9s No casualties Trenches in S3) shelled all day. RHB	
"	23.8.16		From 8 to 10 am CATERPILLAR VALLEY, was shelled with salvoes of 5.9s. & few shells went over the Batteries at 3.45pm Batteries slopped with a infantry attack of 2n MUNSTERS, of the remaining portion a barrage of 30 min & configuration in our 5.45. Up to zero hour 18pdr Batteries fired 3 gpds per hour from ZERO fired wr +1 hour. they fired 320 Rds. each. 4.5 hows fire from -2 hours bzero.2hoRaw	
"	24.8.16		hostile Artillery active on CATERPILLAR VALLEY with 5.9s and 8" PMB. At 11.15 am to 12.30 pm Batteries very heavily shelled with 5.9s and 8" about 50 pds per minute. B72 1 gun knocked out D72 1 man killed C72 3 wounded. B72 1 man slightly wounded. In the evening enemy shelled again B72 1 man killed. 3 wounded ORB. the Batteries (RMB) 1 KILLED 8"	
"	25.8.16		In the evening the enemy shelled the Batteries with 8"	
	27.8.16			

WAR DIARY
or
INTELLIGENCE SUMMARY
(Erase heading not required.)

Army Form C. 2118

Place	Date	Hour	Summary of Events and Information	Remarks and references to Appendices
MAMETZ	27 8/10	—	Very quiet morning at mid day the enemy had a concentrated shoot on MAMETZ lasted with 5.9s and 4.2s for about 10 minutes. This was repeated at 6 P.M.	PMB
	28 8/10	—	At 3.15 am the Relief of the 3rd J. Bde (1st Div) by 46 J Bde (15 Div) was completed. The 72nd Bde now covers part of 46 J Bde front. We have Liaison Officer at Right Battalion H.Q. The day and night were quiet.	PMB
	29 8/10		Special operations supposed to have been carried out were cancelled. Quiet day nothing to report. Weather extremely wet.	PMB
	30 8/10		Hostile artillery active against our trenches in S.3c and D between 3 P.M. and 5 P.M. The BAZENTIN ridge was shelled intermittently during the afternoon and night. In the early hours of the morning the infantry captured that part of the intermediate trench remaining in the hands of the enemy in S.2c taking 4 officers & N.C.O.s 127 men.	
	31 8/10		During the day the enemy shelled ridge at S.26A and B with 4.2s and 5.9s from direction of COURCELETTE. Communications to the Batteries broken 6 times. and a little shrapnel over the Batteries. During the night the enemy put over a good many Gas Shells into the Batteries.	

Total Casualties:
- 1 Officer Killed
- 1 " Wounded (at duty)
- 6 O.R. Killed
- 23 Wounded
- 13 " (at duty)

HONOURS and REWARDS.
- No 58 663 Sgt. HEWITT. E.g.)
- No 86 671 Bomb. EGGINS. S.) MILITARY. MEDAL.
- No 58 663 a Bomb. BLUNDEN. C. (

J.W. Stirling Lt. Col. RFA.
Comg. 72 Bde RFA.

To Headquarters
15th Divl Arty
                        Confidential

    Herewith War Diary Vol 14 for month of September.
    Duplicate has been forwarded to Records.

                      N. Butcher.   Lieut for
                                      Captain R.F.A.
                    Commanding 72nd Brigade, R.F.A.

2 10/16

CONFIDENTIAL.

War Diary

of

72nd Brigade Royal Field Arty

From 1st September, 1916 to 30th September, 1916.

Volume Number 14

E Boyce

Major, R.A.
Bde Major 15th Divisional Arty.

Army Form C. 2118

WAR DIARY
or
INTELLIGENCE SUMMARY
(Erase heading not required.)

VOL No.

Instructions regarding War Diaries and Intelligence Summaries are contained in F. S. Regs., Part II. and the Staff Manual respectively. Title Pages will be prepared in manuscript.

Place	Date	Hour	Summary of Events and Information	Remarks and references to Appendices
MAMETZ.	1.9/16.		Batteries shelled with gas shells in the early hours of the morning. From 9.45am to 12noon A72 and B72 heavily shelled with 5.9s and 4.2s. 3 guns of B72 knocked out. 1 man A72 killed. RH.B.	
	2.9/16		Fairly quiet day. The enemy shelled the ridge behind BAZENTIN le GRAND with 4.2s during the afternoon. The B Batteries were shelled with gas shells for 4 hours during the night. (About 2/L Ticket and 3 men gassed. The Relief of A72 is now in root RH.B. o A72 by B70 completed)	
	3.9/16.		Today attacks took place all along the line. 1st D.A. supported the 7th div in their attack on HIGH WOOD. Attack started at 12noon. Our Batteries carried out Barrages in accordance with orders from 15.D.A. The attack was successful on the right but did not go well in centre or left. In the evening the enemy counter-attacked and we are now on our old line. RH.B.	
	4.9/16		Quiet all day. At 7pm the enemy put up a heavy barrage in our front and support line in S.3.c and D. S.O.S. rockets were sent up but no infantry attack followed. RH.B.	
	5.9/16		Another quiet day. Enemy shelled CATERPILLAR VALLEY slightly during the afternoon also overtrenches in S.2.D. On our right the enemy are putting up a heavy barrage between DELVILLE and HIGH WOOD. RH.B.	
	6.9/16		The trenches in S.3.c and D shelled intermittently during today from the direction of FAUCOURT L'ABBAYE. Are hostile Aeroplane brought down in the evening. A very quiet day.	
	7.9/16		Hostile artillery again quiet against Battery positions. The trenches in S.3.c and D at 6 pm the 1st div attacked HIGH WOOD and the trench found. All Batteries carried out programme in conjunction with the attack operations. This attack was not a success in S.3.B - S3.a - S.3.A also S.3.B - S.3.J - S.3.A.
	8.9/16.		The enemy put up a heavy barrage in all places.	

Army Form C. 2118

WAR DIARY
or
INTELLIGENCE SUMMARY
(Erase heading not required.)

Instructions regarding War Diaries and Intelligence Summaries are contained in F.S. Regs., Part II. and the Staff Manual respectively. Title Pages will be prepared in manuscript.

Place	Date	Hour	Summary of Events and Information	Remarks and references to Appendices
MAMETZ	9/9/16		The attacks on HIGH WOOD was repeated starting at 4.45 pm. Batteries of 72 Bde took part in preliminary bombardment also in the barrage during the attack. This time it is burnt to capture some of the trenches on the right of the wood viz Cough wood. The enemy put up the same barrage as before.	
	10/9/16		Very quiet day. In the evening after 5-9 in S.20.B. no casualties in 72 Bde RFA.	
X.21.C SUNKEN VALLEY	11/9/16		72 Bde relieved the 251 Bde RFA. in this position. Relief complete by 12 NOON. Bde Hqrs and Batteries went close in X21c and X14A. Orders received from 16 want Toronto 12 war to relieve 235. Bde RFA. RAB.	
BOTTOM WOOD X.29.A.2.5.	12/9/16		Bde Hqr and Batteries got orders over to position in X23D. Hqr in Bottom Wood, in relief of 235 Bde RFA 47 Bn guns were changed. Gods Shelling without ordinary. RAB. 72 Bn now of group chose up of Bde C72 D72	B70 D71
"	13/9/16		Batteries carried out bombardments according to programme from 15 DA. The Trenches in RAB	B71 C72 D72
"	14/9/16		S.D. heavily shelled throughout the day. Quiet day.	
"	15/9/16		Programme carried out as ordered. 15 Div attacked at 6.20 am. At 8-6-15 Tanks went over. W/Tanks a great success. The enemy completely taken by surprise. By 7.15 Stfselow gained at 7.10 B72 fired on the retreating enemy on to FANCOURT LABBAYE Rd. 9.20 all firing ceased. 9.40 All Batteries of owed on FA27. and M.27.B. At 10.15 the Tanks still seen on every group. 11.33 Jerry troops with was spread on over the front this Som enemy. 12.25 New target for the Batteries M27 B 47½ - M27 C 29 - M27 D 81 ½. Huns MILL and PORK Pie in M27 E. A great place of enemy movement was seen between 1 pm and 4 pm. The Sw Ba in about wight give taken HIGH WOOD and the Canadians under left their objective 5 pm 15 Dw have taken MARTINPUICH. B72 C72 and D71 went through at 7 pm. A counter attack was expected at 7.45 pm. All quiet at 8 pm. Quiet night.	RAB
"	16/9/16		Barrages according to 16 DA orders carried out 8 pm. B70. D72 moved forward. PAB	
"	17/9/16		A Quiet day except for shelling of MARTINPUICH and its vicinity by enemy. Barrage S.B/MARTINPUICH RAB of the Canadians acted by Enemy put up a desperate attempt to Enemy pouch RAB	

WAR DIARY
or
INTELLIGENCE SUMMARY
(Erase heading not required.)

Army Form C. 2118

Place	Date	Hour	Summary of Events and Information	Remarks and references to Appendices
BOTTOM WOOD X29A25.	18/9/16		Hostile Artillery quiet during the morning and afternoon. In the evening he put up a heavy barrage from COURCELETTE to HIGH WOOD in defence against the Canadian attack on our Right. D71 silenced a battery in M15B,6,3. During the night at 12.45 N and 3 am. R.S shell was fired into M29.21. PMB	
	19/9/16		The weather is bad. The enemy were found to be in a trench in M26B and pressed to come over. This was therefore bombarded with 18 pdrs and 4.5 Hows. Gas shells were again fired into M21A at 12.45 am and 3.15 am. The hostile artillery fairly quiet although it appears that he is bringing up guns again having taken them all back the day MARTINPUICH was taken. Orders received that the Div is to be relieved tomorrow by 23rd Div. PMB	
BOTTOM WOOD and ST GRATIEN	20/9/16		Quiet day. Relief taking place all complete by 3pm. A72 which has been in rest for past 10 days came up and relieved A75. B72. C72. D72 HQ. RHA. 104 Bde RFA. PMB.	
	21/9/16 to 22/9/16		ST GRATIEN to rest. Weather still bad. Div. in rest.	
	23/9/16		Quiet day. Nothing to report. 29.9.16. Col. Jas Sterling went on leave and Capt. J Fairgrieve took command RHA	
			In rest.	
			Honors and rewards during the month: Officers. Nil. O.R. Sgt. F. Miles. B72. DCM. " Blanton C72. " L. ffrench. A72. Spr. Slliestin Nilkerton " J.Williams " Duckins Bmr Turner S. Hallyson P.B. Middleton MILITARY MEDAL	
			Total casualties for the month Officers. 1. Wounded (Gas) (at duty) " 1 " " O.R. 2 Killed 4 Wounded (Gas) 4 Wounded.	PMB J Fairgrieve Capt RFA Cmdg 72 Bde RFA

1875 Wt. W593/826 1,000,000 4/15 J.B.C. & A. A.D.S.S./Forms/C. 2118.

CONFIDENTIAL.

War Diary

of

71 Bde RFA

1st October, 1916.   to   31st October, 1916.

VOLUME. 16

[signature] Boyce

Major R.A.

Brigade Major 15th Divisional Arty.

Army Form C. 2118

Vol 16

WAR DIARY
or
INTELLIGENCE SUMMARY Vol 16
(Erase heading not required.)

Instructions regarding War Diaries and Intelligence Summaries are contained in F.S. Regs., Part II. and the Staff Manual respectively. Title Pages will be prepared in manuscript.

Place	Date	Hour	Summary of Events and Information	Remarks and references to Appendices
ST GRATIEN	1.10.16		Still in Rest Billets Nothing to Report. PM3	
	2.10.16		" " " " " "	
	3.10.16		In rest - A72 came out of action and rejoined the Bde in Rest PM3	
	4.10.16		" - nothing to report PM3	
	5.10.16		" - Lt W Stirling RFA returned from leave PM3	
	6.10.16		" - Received orders to go up into action. 8" PM3	
	7.10.16			
LOWER WOOD X18 A 95	8.10.16		Moved up and relieved 102 Bde Bde in action. 18 pdr Bty's W of HIGH WOOD. 4.5 How in MARTINPUICH day a little hostile shelling PM3	
	9.10.16		Barrage was kept up by day and night on enemy front line and support lines. An S.O.S. was sent through at 12 mdr all guns active again at 12.30 am (11-10-16) hostile artillery active in MARTINPUICH and M 33C during the day. VILLA SMITH MAISON was shelled during the night with 5-9's PM3	
	10.10.16			
	11.10.16		Ordinary Barrage carried out - Special Test Barrage opened at 3.15pm and 5.35pm the evening retaliated at once nothing further to report PM3	
	12.10.16		Ordinary barrage kept up from 7am - ZERO at 2.5pm when the Division on our right (9th Div) carried out an attack on the MARTINPUICH-BUTTE de (WARLENCOURT L'ANGLE (15 Div) went down a defensive flank with BAPAUME Ra. The attack was not successful & All S/B's their old front line. At 10.30 am S/B's was shelled 1 gun knocked out - 5 men were killed & 1 wounded. The night passed off without incident. PM3	
	13.10.16		Barrage kept up as usual. Nothing to report. Hostile artillery active MARTINPUICH	
	14.10.16		Usual day and night barrage kept up also bombarded GUNPITS trench during the evening and a battery in M5A was engaged and believe put. LITTLE WOOD was fired on twice during the day. Our hostile enemy artillery quiet PM3	

1875 Wt. W593/826 1,000,000 4/15 J.B.C.&A. A.D.S.S./Forms/C.2118.

WAR DIARY or INTELLIGENCE SUMMARY

Army Form C. 2118

(Erase heading not required.)

Instructions regarding War Diaries and Intelligence Summaries are contained in F. S. Regs., Part II. and the Staff Manual respectively. Title Pages will be prepared in manuscript.

Place	Date	Hour	Summary of Events and Information	Remarks and references to Appendices
15A.9.5.	15.10.16	—	Barrages were kept up day and night on the enemys front and support line by Batteries, a Special Centreplane forward men was carried out to test the accuracy of the S.O.S. barrage. AA & LA Artillery fairly quiet. Hostile aircraft very active all day. PMS.	Group Reference
	16.10.16	—	Barrages kept up as usual. WARLENCOURT was bombarded by the R.G.A. Hostile Artillery Quiet. Aircraft again active and considerable movement was seen throughout the day on the HEBUT-BAPAUME Rd. PMS.	See LIGNY-THILLOY MAP. 1/10000
	17.10.16		Barrages kept up night and day. A suspected MG. was shelled by Batteries with good results to Sunken Rd in M5a 33 was shelled. Observation was difficult battery owing to the bad mist Section of A72 was detailed by Corps for anti aircraft at low altitude battery to observe 2 hostile aeroplanes. PMS. and averaged
	18.10.16	at 3.40AM two sections of the 9th Div on our left attacked the French from M17 e03 to M18c14. 72" Bde RFA assisted in accordance with 15DA O.O. No 44. Yorkshire barrage and left batteries continued firing a slow rate till 7.40 AM. The operation was partially successful. at 3.30pm May 4.5 How Batteries including D72 Bombarded LOW PART wood for 5 minutes. several fires were observed in the wood otherwise a quiet day. PMS. Hostile Artillery Quiet. LOW PART WOOD was again bombarded at 5 pm. The Barrages were kept up during the Day and night. 9th Div did a small bombing attack at 11.30pm. PMS.	
	19.10.16	Barrages Continued as usual also to BAPAOMETTE in M11B86. The Prussian M11D33 & M11c64 and 45.9 at M11B9466 were engaged for the 1st Day running. LOW PART WOOD was again bombarded by the "Heavies" and 45 Hows. 9th Div did another bombing attack at 4pm. PMS	
	20.10.16			
	21.10.16	The I Corps on our left carried our an attack at 12.6 pm today. 72 Bde did not take part in the bombardment. The enemy retaliated slightly on our front. Reports show that the operation was fairly successful. PMS	
	22.10.16	Very quiet day till 4pm at which hour the enemy opened a heavy barrage between M22.B. 3.7.½ to N23 A.9.14. which continued to 5pm. Barrages continued as usual by batteries.	

WAR DIARY

Army Form C. 2118

Place	Date	Hour	Summary of Events and Information	Remarks and references to Appendices
LONGUEVAL XIEa 9.5.	23.10.16		At 2.30pm the enemy put up a heavy barrage on our front and on our right. It emanated from FAUCOURT L'ABBAYE through the cutting in M.16c 67 & 5&rs. It lasted for 3½ hour during which time DESTREMONT FARM was also shelled. 1 section of Bty went forward (approx 6-M33 c 88. Batteries carried on with its programme of continual bombardment. RMS	
	24.10.16 25.10.16		A very heavy quiet and rain all day. Bombardment continued. Quiet day. RMS Hostile Artillery active. Against LE SARS. FAUCOURT L'ABBAYE, and country in between. About 7AM the Australian Div on our left attacked. Nothing further to report. RMS	
	26.10.16		Hostile Artillery very active during the afternoon on the roads in rear of front line. Freuburg w3 M.27 c 28. M.33 B.D. Battery's carried usual barrage. RMS	
	27.10.16		Hostile artillery quiet during the morning. At 4.30 pm after the enemy had sent up many red lights his Artillery opened a heavy barrage on our front and support line from L=SARS 6 BODECOURT. This lasted 1½ hrs 5pm. Batteries opened fire on S.O.S. lines. Enemy Lights out weather bad. Day and night. Barrage kept up. RMS	
	28.10.16		Quiet day except for some shelling of the Light Railway at M.344. Day and night barrage kept up. Or 10 am 372 Bat. put in a creeping barrage from in front of Battery position to behind his support line. RMS	
	29.10.16		LE SARS and FAUCOURT L'ABBAYE and MARTINPUICH were shelled during the day S 72 gun in a bombardment of LITTLE WOOD M.10 c 051 at 12 MN. 28/29th with 6IN shells. RMS	
	30.10.16 31.10.16		Very quiet day. Nothing to Report. Hostile Artillery fairly quiet. Barrage when issued day and night. 3 Special shoots were carried out of the enemy trenches. RMS	
			Casualties during the month: Officers NIL. O.R. Killed 5 Wounded 9.	Honours and Rewards. Officers Lieut. FAIRGRIEVE. MC O.R. DCM 1 BARS " 1 MILITARY MEDAL 16

CONFIDENTIAL.

War Diary.

of

[handwritten: 73rd Bde R.F.A.]

From 1st November, 1916 - 30th November, 1916.

VOLUME __16__

1.11.16.   *[signature]* Captain,
                        for Bd Major 15th Divisional Arty.

Confidential

To Headquarters
15th Divl Arty

Herewith War Diary Vol 17 for month of November

R.H. Bingham
Colonel, R.F.A.
Commanding 72nd Brigade, R.F.A.

30/1/16

Army Form C. 2118

Vol 17

WAR DIARY
or
INTELLIGENCE SUMMARY   Vol. 17
(Erase heading not required.)

Place	Date	Hour	Summary of Events and Information	Remarks and references to Appendices
LOWER WOOD HIER 95	1.11.16		Hostile Artillery quiet during the morning. The Enemy opened a heavy barrage on our line from LE SARS - FAVCOURT, L'ABBAYE. PAB	
	2.11.16		Hostile Battery quiet during the morning and active again in the afternoon, fire opened again at 12.15pm. Artillery carried out ordinary Day and Night Barrages. PAB A front and very light show on the BAPAUME Rd at MIERS. PAB	
	3.11.16		Hostile Artillery very quiet during the day. Normal Day and Night Barrage carried out as usual. PAB	
	4.11.16		Hostile Artillery more active during the day. Our 1st and 2nd Gps. fire put up a Hostile Bde from LE SARS to KNOCOURT L'ABBAYE. The heavy firing on our Bde front Canadians on our left attacked. PAB	
	5.11.16		To day at 9.10 am the 50th Div on our right attacked assisted by 15DA. New Battalions fire barrage according to orders. 15Dn RM Bde. The Division gained its objective but had to retire later. PAB	
	6.11.16 7.11.16		Carried n/r usual barrage. PAB PAB Batteries shelled with 8" for 1 hour. No casualties. PAB	
	8.11.16		1st Section of each Battery. A.B & C 72. were relieved by. 2nd sections of ABee 73. PAB	
St GRATIEN	9.11.16		Remainder of Bde relieved by 73rd Bde. Relief completed by 2pm. Bde marched into Rest at ST GRATIEN. PAB	
	10.11.16 11.11.16		In Rest - PAB PAB	

Army Form C. 2118

WAR DIARY
or
INTELLIGENCE SUMMARY
(Erase heading not required.)

Instructions regarding War Diaries and Intelligence Summaries are contained in F.S. Regs., Part II. and the Staff Manual respectively. Title Pages will be prepared in manuscript.

Place	Date	Hour	Summary of Events and Information	Remarks and references to Appendices
PIERREGOT	12.11.16		The Brigade marched to PIERREGOT about 4 miles N. of about not filled in Rect. Nothing to report. The Bde was billeted by Major Gen. McCracken G.O.C. 15. Div.	PH3
	13.11.16		"	PH3
	14.11.16		"	
	15.11.16		Received news that a new battery from England was coming to join the Bde.	PH3
	16.11.16		532" Howitzer Battery arrived at 9am. Gunmen did by Capt. Graham. M.E. Rfa.	PH3
	17.11.16		The whole Brigade (A.B.C.572) was inspected by the C.O.	PH3
	18.11.16		Nothing to report	PH3
	19.11.16		1 Section of each battery moved up into the line in relief of Batteries of 70th Bde Rfa.	PH3
	20.11.16		Remaining Section moved up.	PH3
CONTALMAISON VILLA	21.11.16		H.q. moved up and took over from 70th Bde Rfa at CONTALMAISON VILLA X11.5.9. Pall. light & hatman: map. Batteries are billeted. A/2. M32.c.6.2. B/2. S2.a.4.9. C/2. M32.c.8.4. with one Anti-tank Gun at M27.c.0.6. D/70 also came under 72 Bde Rfa. D/72 having remained in the line all this time. Its remainder of the Bde were at rest at about 6.30 p.m. a 5.9 shell fell into the entrance of one of B/72. gun pits damaging the gun and wounding 1 Sgt and 2 men and 1 man badly wounded died.	PH3
" "	22.11.16		MARTINPUICH shelled with 8" Nothing to report.	PH3
" "	23.11.16		Quiet day. Weather v. bad.	PH3
" "	24.11.16		Nothing to report.	PH3
" "	25.11.16		"	PH3
" "	26.11.16		Hostile artillery more active than usual. MARTINPUICH shelled as usual.	PH3
" "	27.11.16		Quiet day.	
" "	28.11.16		Batteries carried out 7 short bursts of S.O.S. lines during the 24 hours.	PH3
" "	29.11.16		" " " " " " "	PH3
" "	30.11.16		Quiet day. Nothing to report.	PH3

Honours. B.S.M. Furman. Military Medal.
S/S since died of wounds

Brig. [signature] R.F.A
Comdg 72nd Bde R.F.A

30/11/16

CONFIDENTIAL

WAR DIARY

of

72nd Brigade R.F.A.

From 1st December, 1916 to 31st December, 1916.

VOLUME 17

[signature]
Major, R.A.
Brigade Major 15th Divisional Artillery.

WAR DIARY
or
INTELLIGENCE SUMMARY

(Erase heading not required.)

Army Form C. 2118

Vol 18 (cont)

Place	Date	Hour	Summary of Events and Information	Remarks and references to Appendices
CONTALMAISON VILLA	1.12.16		Reorganisation of 15"S.A. started. A.B.C.72 became A72 and B72. C72 split up to make another two Batteries 6 guns each. A72 commanded by Capt. C.E. Russell, B72 by Capt. AT.G. Gardner. Captains A72. Capt. J.E.M. Hoskyn. B72. Lt. A. Butcher. Remains the same under Capt. J. Fairgrieve. Batteries and H.Q. whole of MARTINPUICH very heavily shelled from 7.30pm - 10.30pm with S.9 & 4.2. 77mm. Our gas shell barrage. PMS	
	2.12.16		Quiet day. Reorganisation in the Bde complete. Battery positions not shelled by the Bosche (except another gas shell barrage at night on MARTINPUICH. PMS	
	3.3.16		Bde H.Q. moved to LOWER WOOD Batteries remain the same. C70 comes under command of 72 Bde R.F.A. D72 still in rest. A very successful raid carried out. Artillery active on our front area. EAUCOURT L'ABBAYE. Imports to M17. PM3	
	4.3.16		Hostile Artillery active. PM3	
	5.3.16		Quiet day.	
	6.3.16		Hostile Artillery active.	
	7.3.16		Hostile Battery active on our trenches. Bar 709.	
	8.3.16		Quiet day. Nothing to report on LE BARS and EAUCOURT L'ABBAYE PM3	
LOWER WOOD (X15 A 5.9.)	9-12-16		— do —	PM3
	10-12-16		— do —	113
	11-12-16		— do —	113
	12-12-16		D/72nd relieved D/40d on M.32 & 34	
	13-12-16		dies up very quiet, nothing of importance to report. 113	
	14-12-16			
	15-12-16		Misty day, nothing of importance to report	113
	16-12-16			

Army Form C. 2118.

WAR DIARY
or
INTELLIGENCE SUMMARY

(Erase heading not required.)

Vol. 18 (cont)

Place	Date	Hour	Summary of Events and Information	Remarks and references to Appendices
LOWER WOOD (X17 A 5.9)	17.12.16		XI of D.A.H.Q. relieved 45th D.A.H.Q. at 10 a.m., very misty, nothing of importance to report	A13
	18.12.16		Very misty, nothing of importance to report	A13
	19.12.16			
	20.12.16		Observation good today, enemy's aircraft very active. nothing of importance to report.	A13
	21.12.16		Quiet day. Nothing to report. W.K.L. Maj. P.T.S. Partner went on leave	
	22.12.16		A72 B72 and Hq 72. being relieved by 71st Bde W.K.L	
	23.12.16		Above relief complete. W.K.L	
	24.12.16		In rest. W.K.L	
	25.12.16		Christmas day In rest.	
	26.12.16		In rest. C.O's lecture B all officers. W.K.L	
PIERREGOT	27.12.16		In " " " Nothing to Report P.T.S	
"	28.12.16		" " " C.O lecture B all officers and 15 N.C.O. per Battery P.T.S	
"	29.12.16		" " " of Divisional School Capt. Butcher lecture 15 1/Pdr Offrs. per Battery P.T.S	
"	30.12.16		" " " Lecture by Capt S.D Staff A.V.C. Offrs 15th coy bombardiers P.T.S	
"	31.12.16		" " " Church Parade and Inspection Vy. P.t.o P.T.S	
			Casualties Wounds and Rounds. Nil	
			40 R wounded	
			4 died of wounds	

J.W. Stirling
Lt. Col. R.F.A
– Comg 72 Bde R.F.A

www.ingramcontent.com/pod-product-compliance
Lightning Source LLC
Chambersburg PA
CBHW081552160426
43191CB00011B/1908